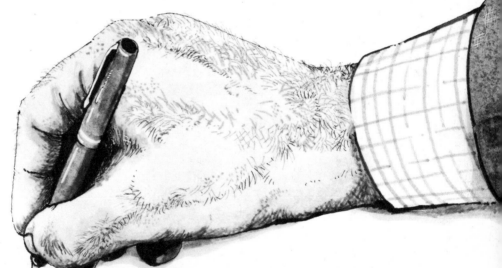

DO~IT~YOURSELF
BRAIN
SURGERY

To Jeff Chandler,
without whom there
would be
fewer pictures
in this book

DO~IT~YOURSELF BRAIN SURGERY

& OTHER HOME SKILLS

Stewart Cowley

a Charles Herridge book
published by

Frederick Muller Limited
London NW2 6LE

First published in Great Britain in 1981
by

Frederick Muller Limited
London NW2 6LB

Reprinted 1981 (twice)

Produced by Charles Herridge Ltd
Tower House, Abbotsham, Devon
Designed (well, sort of) by
Bruce Aiken and Colin Rowe .
Typeset by Toptown Printers Ltd
Printed by The Pitman Press, Bath

ISBN - 0 584 97073 0 (cased edition)
ISBN - 0 584 97104 4 (limp edition)

CONTENTS

INTRODUCTION

Dear Do-It-Yourselfer

In the field of Do-It-Yourself, those most deeply committed are
a breed apart from their fellows, and it is to them rather than
to those who wield an occasional hammer to drive their thumbs into
the woodwork that this book is addressed. Theirs is the pioneer
spirit, which encourages man to plunge into the unknown in search
of an ideal; to strive to grasp what lies just beyond his normal
reach; to commit himself to fate and fortune with his eyes firmly
fixed on a distant and unexplored horizon.

This is the spirit that marks the difference between the man who
devotes a free afternoon to flicking a fresh coat of paint on the
front door, and the one who sets out to build his own offshore oil
rig armed only with a few lengths of steel pipe, scrap metal, an
electric drill and a rubber dinghy. It is a question of attitude as
much as of application, and the cream of the Do-It-Yourself fraternity
tend to be born, not made.

This book will help you to cultivate these qualities as well as set you
on the road to devising your own advanced Do-It-Yourself projects,
but, having decided that you possess the necessary spiritual qualities,
there are other background considerations which need to be borne in
mind. One of the most important of these is safety, of ensuring, so
far as is possible, your survival.

Accidents can and will happen and it is vital for you to know the
basic principles of first aid. Stand in front of a large mirror and
take a good look at your body. Notice how many bits of it stick out
and familiarize yourself with them all, so that you will be able to
make quick checks at periodic intervals to make certain that you are
still intact and undamaged. Note also the location of all joints and
flexing points, particularly along the arms and legs. If, during the
course of a project, you notice that these limbs are bending at other
points there is a very good chance that they have broken.

In the case of punctures, cuts or tears in the skin, try to effect
temporary repairs as quickly as possible to prevent them becoming
worse. The skin plays a vital role in keeping the body together and
too severe a rupture in its surface can allow the contents to fall
out. You will be amazed at just how much fits inside the human body.
Once a large proportion has fallen out it can become quite unmanageable
and exremely difficult to fit back correctly.

Any injury of this kind will involve the loss of blood, and the import
importance of this substance makes it doubly essential to effect repairs
immediately. Never attempt to top up with a transfusion after a
spillage unless you have a supply of the exact type and classification
used in your body as you could do more harm than good. The body is a
very delicate piece of equipment and will not function on anything less
than an exact match. Look after it as well as you would any of your
other tools, and always give it a quick wash down after use to maintain
its condition.

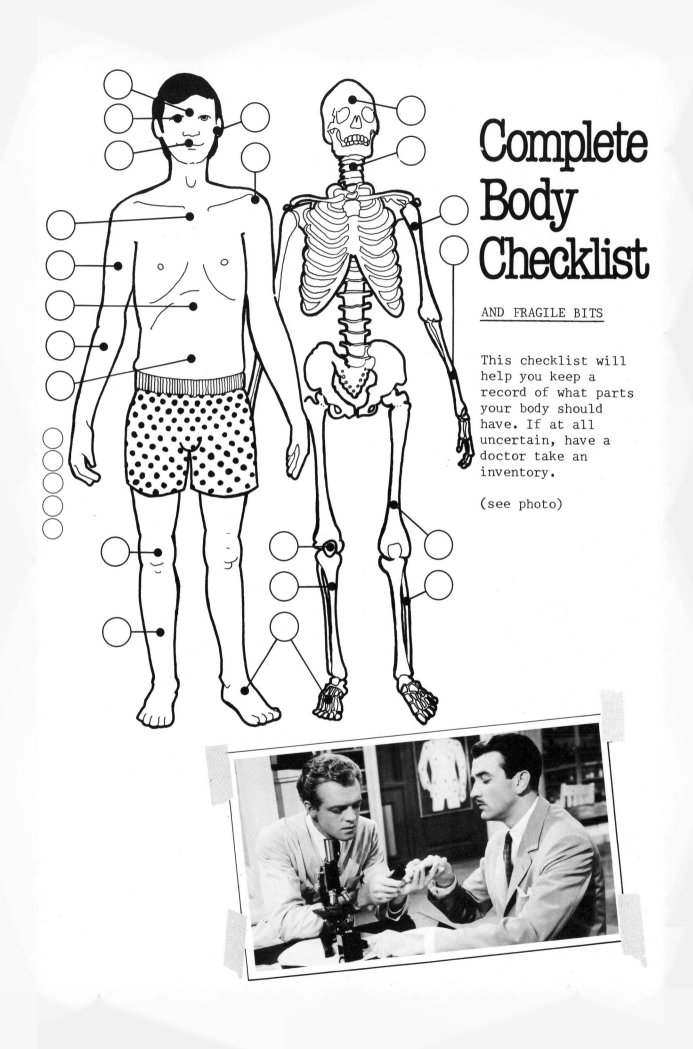

Complete Body Checklist

<u>AND FRAGILE BITS</u>

This checklist will help you keep a record of what parts your body should have. If at all uncertain, have a doctor take an inventory.

(see photo)

When actually working, do not permit your body to operate for long periods in exreme temperatures as its performance will soon deteriorate. It might also suffer long-term damage that is difficult or expensive to correct. Falling off things, particularly very high things, must be avoided at all costs, and the same applies to letting things, particularly very heavy things, fall on you. The effect in both instances is very similar and will at best cause considerable delays in the progress of your work. Breathing is also terribly important, particlarly when working underwater, so never become so absorbed in your work that you neglect this aspect of your body's requirements.

Always have a comprehensive repair or first-aid kit at hand when work ing as this can make all the differnce in surviving an accident. How comprehensive this is will depend largely on cost, and your local doctor will be able to advise you on assembling the most effective kit for a given price range.

Prevention is, however, infinitely better than cure, and you can do much to minimize the risk of an accident by adopting various procedural principles in your working methods. Always try, for example, to avoid running into sharp and pointed objects which may penetrate the skin, and never precipitate movement in large heavy objects without ensuring that your anatomy is well clear. When working at considerable heights always make sure that you have a safety line secured to a solid fixture. Remember that it is not enough to tie yourself to an object that is not itself fixed unless it is several times your own body weight, as you might find that in falling you simply bring it with you, with the attendant risk of compounding the injuries sustained as a direct result of the fall.

Burns are another common source of injury and are yet more difficult to cope with once sustained. Do not let yourself get into bad habits such as placing a lit welding torch behind your ear or in your pocket when not actually in use. Do not light matches to read labels on crates of explosives when underground and never keep powerful acids or chemical mixtures in your vacuum flask without a label. If you grade each day's activities according to their risk and spend a few moments contemplating their dangers, you should find it easy to avoid being taken by surprise.

Follow these basic rules and there is no reason why any of the projects described here should present dangers. Remember that a cool head is the best remedy. Standing and screaming in desperate panic is not helpful.

It remains only to say that there will almost certainly be times when you may doubt the wisdom of tackling one of the more difficult projects, these are the occaions when your reserves of perseverance, strength and indomitability must be called upon if you are to become one of the Do-It-Yourself elite. If you possess these qualities and can disregard the taunts and disparagements fm of your lesser fellows you will find yourself embarking on a new era of excitement, fulfilment and enlightenment in your life.

Good luck.

pp. Stewart Cowley

dictated by Mr Cowley but signed in his absence

↑
If you get superglue on your hands,
keep them away from your face.

↑
In fact, if you get
superglue on your hands,
do not touch anything.

← Don't get over-confident.
Bengt Soderstrom got this
far building an aircraft,
then spoilt everything by
grazing his knuckles when
the wrench slipped (just
after this picture was
taken) and dying of
tetanus the next day.

MULTIPLY YOUR FRIENDS WITH HOME CLONING

You will need

Assorted culture dishes
Incubator
Rubber tubing, pipettes and a retort
8 x 2lb jars of genetic jelly
Microscope
Bicycle pump
2 lbs best steak

Before You Start

Wash your hands
Put out your cigarette

There are few things in life more exciting than being in the forefront of scientific discovery, leading the struggle to unravel the profound mysteries of nature and exploit them in the service of your fellow beings. The first difficulty is finding a brand-new field where the lack of competition will allow you to gain the advantage, and one such field is that of genetics. Our growing understanding of the processes involved is creating a wealth of commercial opportunities, one of the most dramatic being the principle of cloning, a branch of genetic engineering. Cloning is the experimental process whereby organic cells can be reconstructed to produce an exact duplicate of the parent organism. Imagine the potential that exists if this process is applied to the human body! The applications for carbon-copy people are endless and provide immense scope for the entrepreneur. With a little hard work and ingenuity you could revolutionize the field of high security; providing decoy doubles, indistinguishable from the real thing, perfect stand-ins for movie stars, for businessmen taking long trips away from their families, and so on.

There are a few basic principles that you will need to become familiar with in order to begin producing your 'identical doubles', as well as certain key terms. Learn to say a selection of these words until you can introduce them into your conversations with prospective customers without faltering. The best thing to do is to stand in front of a mirror, repeating each word with increasing rapidity until it trips neatly off your tongue. Try, for example, the word Meiosis. Start with your lips together and make a soft humming sound, then allow the bottom jaw to drop open slightly and complete the first syllable by turning the sound into a Y note. Then, without interrupting the flow of sound, open the jaws a little further and bring the lips closer together in a neat circle before stretching them into a sort of

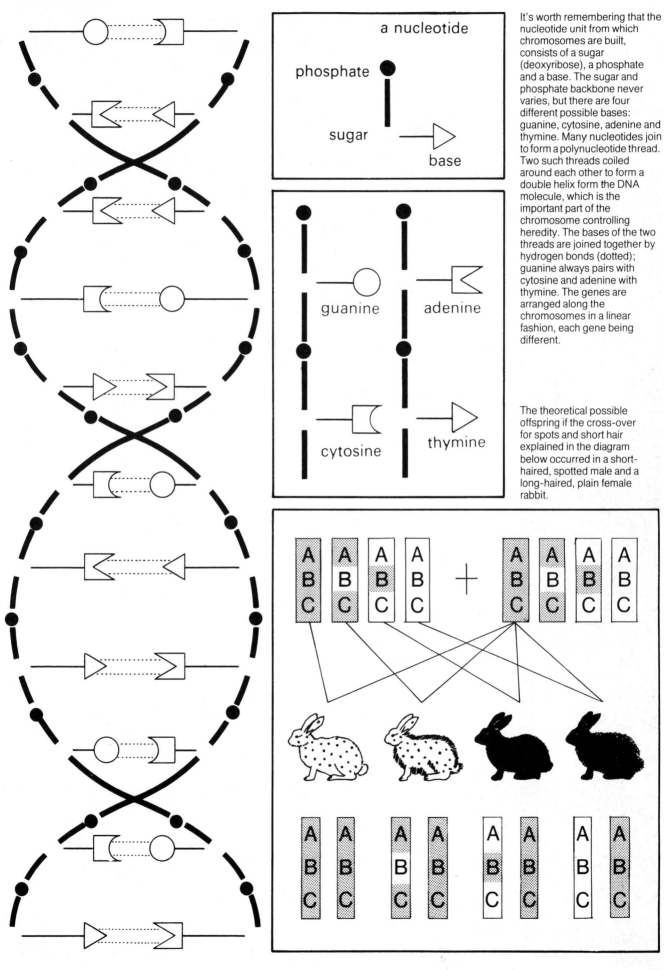

a nucleotide

phosphate ●

sugar ────▷

base

guanine   adenine

cytosine   thymine

It's worth remembering that the nucleotide unit from which chromosomes are built, consists of a sugar (deoxyribose), a phosphate and a base. The sugar and phosphate backbone never varies, but there are four different possible bases: guanine, cytosine, adenine and thymine. Many nucleotides join to form a polynucleotide thread. Two such threads coiled around each other to form a double helix form the DNA molecule, which is the important part of the chromosome controlling heredity. The bases of the two threads are joined together by hydrogen bonds (dotted); guanine always pairs with cytosine and adenine with thymine. The genes are arranged along the chromosomes in a linear fashion, each gene being different.

The theoretical possible offspring if the cross-over for spots and short hair explained in the diagram below occurred in a short-haired, spotted male and a long-haired, plain female rabbit.

If producing more than one clone from an original, do ensure that the genetic material is divided in precisely equal quantities. Inaccurate measuring will produce such unsatisfactory results as these.

Opposite
The very greatest care should always be taken when working with genetic materials. Lack of attention to procedures can lead to grave errors of the kind illustrated here. Always wear apparel made from synthetic materials as natural ones may contain traces of the original genetic substances which can contaminate the cloning process. Here the experimenter's footwear led to a particularly unusual genetic product.

grin for the final hissing syllable. After a few attempts you can confidently introduce this useful word into your vocabulary. Try this technique with other words like chromosome, diploid, Gregor Mendel and fruit fly.

Before actually starting to manipulate genetic codes it is worth taking a close look at one of the basic structures you will be dealing with: the Gene and the vitally important component called DNA. Genes are the fundamental components of heredity and are located among the chromosomes of living tissue. They are extremely hard-wearing and can be washed repeatedly without any appreciable deterioration apart from a slight loss of colouring; a natural phenomenon which is thought highly desirable in certain circles.

DNA, on the other hand, is more delicate, carrying as it does in its fine, intertwined spiral the detailed code that determines the nature of its offspring. It is, quite simply, a double helix bearing units of phosphate and deoxyribose, each of the latter being attached to bases of adenine, thymine, guanine or cytosine whose distribution instructs the protein synthesis site in the cytoplasm through a messenger ribonucleic acid; a polymer of alternating compounds that transcribes the

nucleotide sequences in the genetic deoxynucleic acid. The polymerase RNA enzyme governs the process whereby ribosomal RNA and transfer RNA are synthesized and the specific nucleotide sequence is carried as a linear tape into the ribosome and translated into amino acids by transfer, or decoder RNA, and that's all! There really is no more to it, so roll up your sleeves and try making somebody.

It is probably a good idea to start with quite a small person, on the principle that the smaller the body, the fewer the cells required. For the same reason it is wise to keep things as simple as possible by missing out the bits which make hair, teeth, fingernails, moles, birthmarks and other non-essential details. Later, when you have mastered the general techniques, you can concentrate on the finer points which will give the finished results that touch of extra quality. Although cloning has been widely used for developing certain strains of cereals and vegetables, the cloning of humans is a wide-open field, so try experimenting with various techniques in order to find the method that suits you best.

Take notes as you go along to make sure that you can repeat the process

later. Do remember that cloning is a lengthy process and that there are very few shortcuts, so do not become impatient and the results will reward your self-control. Having prepared the seeds, fertilized them and placed them in the appropriate conditions, you will have to wait for your brand-new person to grow up in the usual way. For this reason it is advisable to start a number of people over a long period so that their development is staggered.

As in any experimental field of research and development you will find that there are plenty of people who will feel able to offer a host of often conflicting suggestions and advice, and who will frequently propose techniques which they themselves swear by. Listen by all means, but relate them to your own experience and do not allow yourself to be rushed into any step that you have not yourself found to be useful.

When utilizing the Vacuum Method of genetic synthesis it is important to make certain that your donor is completely relaxed as any significant degree of muscular tension can inhibit the flow of genes through the skin. In some cases it will also create difficulties in removing the bicycle pump tube from the donor's navel.

Hold the nozzle of the pump with a firm grip when expelling the genetic vapour to avoid scattering it beyond the target area. Genes are very, very tiny and easily mislaid.

A fine example of cloning at its best. All that was required to finish this excellent Valentino clone was minor surgery to separate the fist from the lower jaw.

METHODS

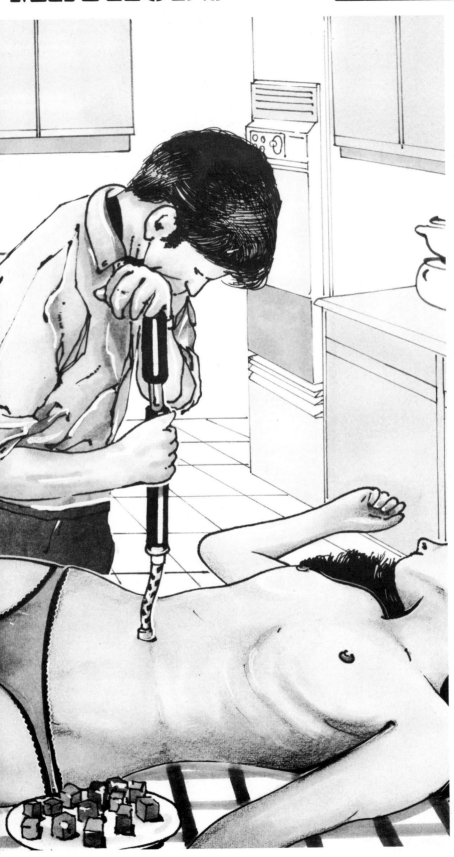

One method which seems currently to be very popular is to lie the subject on a couch or table and bare the midriff, exposing the navel. Wash the immediate area of skin thoroughly with a mild antiseptic solution and place a pillow under the head. Next, take a large plate of good-quality beefsteak diced into small cubes and place it on a chair beside the couch. Insert the nozzle of a bicycle pump in the subject's navel, and with a continuous, fluid motion draw out the handle. When it is fully extended, carefully remove the nozzle and place it well inside the heap of diced meat before gently pressing in the pump handle to expel the gases extracted from your subject. Once this has been done, place the pile of meat in a large kilner jar with enough holes pierced in the lid to ensure an adequate air supply and wait for the duplicate person to grow up.

Whether you intend to duplicate people just for your own amusement or to provide yourself with additional income, remember that patience will be your greatest ally in your quest to revolutionize human society.

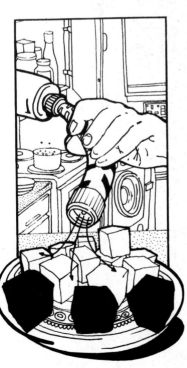

AN OCEAN LINER

2

You will need

A 60ft gantry crane
At least 2 hammers
A wheelbarrow
Lots of Room

The picture shows that unless you have a large garden you should not attempt this project. The *Mauretania*, though less than half the size of the *Queen Mary* shown here, was still a very big boat.

The barest minimum of equipment you will need. Always make sure your tools are laid out neatly as they can easily go astray when working on a large project.

The first decision that the amateur shipbuilder must face is, of course, the choice of vessel, and it is wise to avoid attempting an original design until you have gained some experience. Marine architecture is a highly specialized field and should be approached with caution! Unless you have the necessary qualifications it is far safer to base your project on a tried and proven design, adding minor modifications accord-

ing to taste. But here again there are certain considerations to be borne in mind when making your choice. Some vessels, like that great favourite the *Queen Mary*, are very big ships indeed, and although basic construction techniques are little different from a less ambitious subject, sheer size can prove a problem!

Until you have gained some experience in this field, it is wiser to opt for a medium-sized craft such as those in service in the first part of the century. Vessels such as the *Mauretania* are ideal in that they are not only of a more manageable size but have an important historical appeal, being both fairly modern in construction yet possessing the elegance that was embodied in this golden age of commercial shipping. It is, however, difficult to acquire the plans for ships of this vintage and it will be necessary to undertake a certain amount of preliminary research before beginning the task of construction. Fortunately it is still possible to find photographs and even old picture postcards of these proud ships which can be traced off with the aid of artist's tracing paper and a fairly hard pencil. Remember to take as much care as possible at

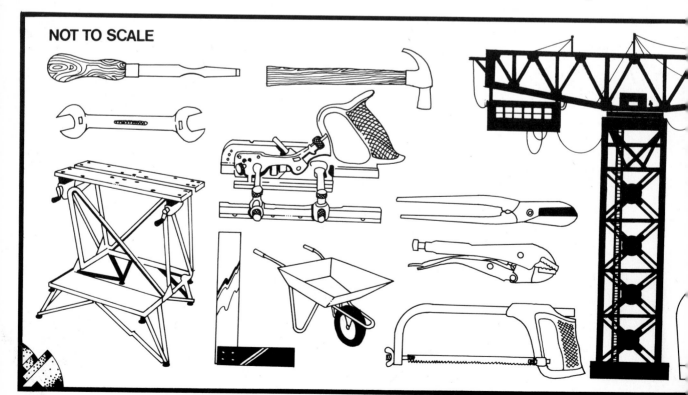

NOT TO SCALE

this stage as a fairly elementary mistake will be magnified in the final construction, and will be hard to correct.

Once you have got your finished tracing you will need to establish at least one true measurement of the original ship in order to establish the scale. It does not matter whether it is the overall length or simply the height of the funnels. Once this has been done, the site should be marked out accordingly to show the basic dimensions and positions of key elements such as engine rooms, bulkheads, position of funnels etc. You are now ready to lay the keel and great care should be taken to make certain it is absolutely straight. There is nothing more frustrating than finally completing a lengthy and laborious replica, meticulous in every detail, only to find that it is banana shaped and only goes round in circles.

You will need arc welding equipment such as that used for submerged arc welding where the process is shielded by a blanket of granular fusible flux. This is the most common method and is recommended for steelwork. Other techniques include inert gas and atomic hydrogen welding but suitable

equipment is more costly with little actual gain unless you intend to try your hand at a wider variety of metalworking projects. Other important items are a large heavy duty crane, a good electric drill for steel plate, a heavy hammer and tongs for riveting, a comprehensive socket set in either Whitworth or metric sizes and as much scaffolding as you can lay your hands on.

Your biggest outlay will undoubtedly be for raw materials. Steel of reasonable quality is fairly expensive but it is not advisable to make use of cheaper alternatives such as fibre-glass for a project of this magnitude. Unless you are a DIY purist and wish to produce your own steel plate and rolled sections you would be better advised to make use of existing suppliers who will deliver direct to the site and may also be willing to provide useful advice as

Attention to contemporary detail can make all the difference, but authenticity need not be expensive to attain. Here the enterprising constructor has used impact adhesive and bottle caps to reproduce the exposed rivets of the original vessel.

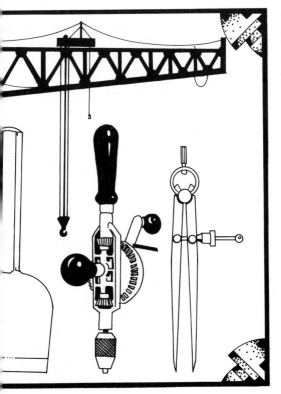

MAURETANIA II

When siting the main props it's advisable to check the ground thoroughly as mine shafts and artesian wells could prove hazardous.

Do beware of trees! What seemed like a small spindly bush at the start of the project can suddenly become a force working against you as the roots work their way under the keel.

If you are lucky enough to be sit near an appartment or office blo this can prove advantageous in many ways.

A small crane can be positioned the roof and will prove invaluab

Having selected your site, begin by pegging out the keel-line. Accuracy during these early stages will avoid having to correct expensive errors later.

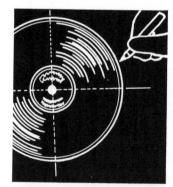

Use an L.P. record to mark out the shape of the portholes for cutting. This will ensure that they are all the same size.

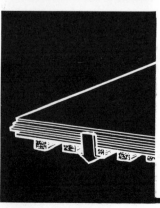

Store steel plates flat to prevent buckling or distorting. Laying them on spaced timbers makes them easy to pick up and will also provide temporary accommodation for the ship's rats until you are ready to transfer them to the finished vessel.

A circular motion when polishing metal surfaces will produce a better shine and reduce the effects of the abrasive action of any cleaning agent.

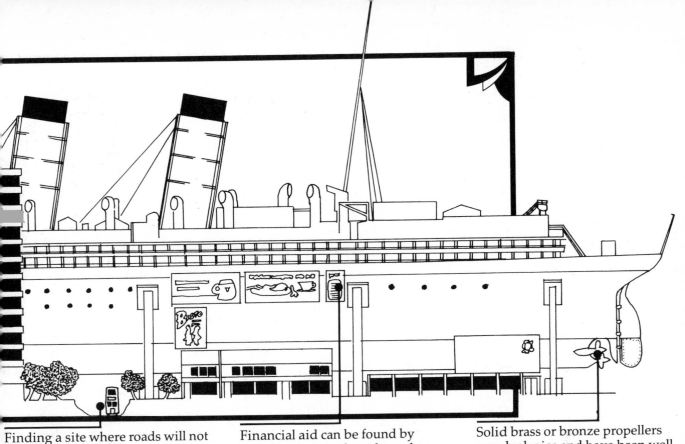

Finding a site where roads will not be obstructed can be difficult and early co-operation with the district authority planners will save many a headache later. These are people you will get to know quite well and you should find them most pleasant and helpful if you get off on the right foot.

Financial aid can be found by hiring out poster boards on the side of your liner. (Be careful not to use adhesives that will mark the paint.)

Solid brass or bronze propellers may look nice and have been well proven but they will provide a temptation to petty thieves and you will be more likely to keep them if made from steel or carbon fibre.

part of their service. Make sure that you have a plentiful supply of rivets, bolts and welding flux to hand as it is easy to overlook these minor items. There is nothing more frustrating than running out of a handful of washers on Sunday and having to halt work until the next weekend.

Although most of the work can be executed alone, there will be times when it will be necessary to enlist the aid of wife or friends for such tasks as lowering hull plates into position. A difficult job becomes easy when there is someone to guide the jib and tack the plate in position until you can take over. Once you have reached this stage you will really begin to feel that your liner is taking shape as the ribs disappear beneath the smooth surface of the hull skin. It will compensate for much of the tedium of endlessly hammering at rivets, but do not be impatient for ensuring that the hull is watertight is

of the utmost importance unless you are building a static replica.

It is better to cut the portholes through once the hull is complete rather than attempt to prefabricate them as this will make the job of positioning them very much easier and will ensure that they are all in straight lines. Nothing spoils a liner so much as crooked porthole lines and the importance of such detailing cannot be over-emphasized. The internal bulkheads and decking should be undertaken before the upper decks and superstructure to permit easy access for the crane, but the degree of complexity will be a matter of personal choice, bearing in mind that internal bracing and supporting sections should not be skimped.

It is also at this stage that the selection of power units should be made. It may be best to take professional advice as to a suitable

To reduce the cost of furnishing your ship in the grand style, it is worth considering building it around some of your more attractive garden trees and shrubs.

A binnacle of the type used on the *Mauretania* It is well worth searching for a few original accessories when fitting out your liner.

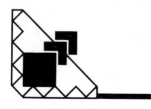

modern replacement for the engines used by the actual ship. The biggest is not necessarily the best and power output must be related to any restrictions dictated by the design of the hull. If you can match the specifications of the original units so much the better, and be certain to test run the installed engines thoroughly before moving on to the next stages, paying particular attention to the torque on the propellor shaft bearing bolts, as excessive vibration can do considerable damage to the units and the hull itself.

When you are satisfied that the drive system is functioning properly you can begin installing the main deck braces and constructing the superstucture. You can make a few economies here by using a thinner gauge steel for the outer skin of the various sections. It may also be worth considering using a synthetic substitute for the decking itself instead of the expensive timberwork of the original *Mauretania*. There will, however, be a detectable difference in finish and texture, particularly once the ship has begun to acquire that sought-after patina of a vintage craft.

The final stage is that of fitting out the ship's systems. You will need plenty of good quality electrical cable so it is worth shopping around for a bulk deal. Most of the main equipment is readily available and will include a reliable and powerful radar system, depthsounders, gyro-compass, etc. It is worth using good quality modern components as they will usually be out of sight and will provide more reliable and up-to-date performance. Some more visible items, however, will pose greater problems. A wheel and binnacle of the correct type and vintage are items which it is important to install to retain the bridge's original charm and these may require a great deal of time and exhaustive searching to locate. Obviously the first places to try are the various breakers' yards, which can prove an exciting source of bits and pieces with which to give your liner that extra touch of authenticity at very reasonable cost. Be prepared to be patient, however, as many hours of fruitless searching are often necessary before that elusive treasure finally turns up.

The proud day when you can stand back and admire the fruits of your efforts, resplendent in her gleaming paintwork and polished brass, will soon arrive and after the ritual of naming and toasting is over you will have to decide your next step; what to do with your noble classic. If you have ready access to the sea then there is little to prevent you from registering, launching and setting off in her, provided that you have succeeded in obtaining your Master's Certificate and purchased the necessary charts for the voyage you have in mind.

Not everyone, however, is fortunate enough to follow this course and some people may have to be satisfied with less. One scheme which has won many followers is to construct a large tank around the ship, using as much of the left-over materials as possible, which is then filled with water to float the vessel. Be prepared for a long wait and enlist the help of your friends if possible in

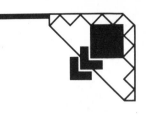

When building a very high liner a good supply of ladders is essential, but make ABSOLUTELY CERTAIN that they are leaning against the ship in the correct fashion. Otherwise, as shown here, anyone on top will be unable to descend to ground level.

order to speed the job up. They are almost certain to oblige just to earn the opportunity of spending some time aboard the great ship!

Whatever your final solution, you are sure to experience that glow of pride in your achievement and the knowledge that you have made some small contribution to our glorious maritime heritage.

To avoid marring the great day with any unfortunate accidents, a useful tip is to place the bottle of champagne inside a small shopping bag or stocking to prevent injuries resulting from flying glass.

You Will Need

A good supply of formaldehyde
A clean handkerchief
Scissors, scalpels or craft knives

Plenty of dead animals
Cotton wool, cardboard, etc.
Glass eyes, matched

Before You Start

Make sure your subject is actually dead. Have plenty of hangers at hand for storing empty skins when not required.

Taxidermy is an ancient craft, probably more ancient than we really recognize. Even the origins of the word are somewhat obscure but we can certainly hazard an educated guess. The definition of the word is the preparation of skins to represent the living animal, but taxi means a conveyance or means of transportation available for general hire, and derm is Latin for skin. We can assume, therefore, that in the very earliest days of the craft (probably in prehistoric times, in view of the lack of surviving examples) the first forms of public transportation took the form of hollowed-out animals in which people could travel. Motive power was probably provided by the owners of the device or their employees, who would operate the limbs. The main advantage of this system may be supposed to be the absence of the necessity to feed or fuel the animal.

It is also reasonable to assume that in order for such a conveyance to be economic, the animal selected would be of the largest practicable size, and this points to the use of various types of dinosaur. Further evidence to support this idea lies in the fact that most of the fossils discovered to date have been of dead animals, which suggests that prehistoric man enjoyed the advantages of a widespread and flourishing system of transportation. Some scientists contest this hypothesis by pointing out that many of the fossils discovered are of creatures too small to have been used in this way, but in reply it is only necessary to point out that the huge number of toy and model cars manufactured today does not disprove the existence of passenger vehicles.

Today we have many alternative and frankly more efficient forms of transport, but the art of taxidermy continues to attract enthusiasts. They are, however, a dwindling band, for the number of practitioners has dropped significantly since the days when almost anything that moved was considered a suitable subject for preservation. Sadly, it is now a dying art. Part of the reason must be the narrow range of subjects usually chosen, and by venturing beyond these limits, the enterprising enthusiast can do much to revitalize this fascinating hobby.

First of all, go for subjects unlikely to be considered by more traditional practitioners, so that you will be free to devise your own

ERMY Stuffing is Fun

Cave drawings of the type shown here would provide conclusive evidence that prehistoric man used empty dinosaurs as a means of transport, thereby inventing the word Taxidermy.

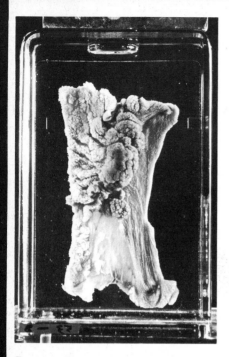

Do not discard those piles of internal organs. With a little thought and ingenuity they can make most attractive decorations and conversation pieces.

methods and break new ground. For example, while it is important to start with easily obtained subjects, it is not necessary to stick to the usual run of garden birds or squirrels. Have a go at houseflies or earthworms, both of which can be mounted in groups in an infinite number of creative and interesting displays. Or alternate the two species and thread them on wire to make original pieces of costume jewelry. Rats, prepared with a suitable rear aperture, make excellent doorhandle covers which are more pleasant to handle than the usual bare metal, *and* they can be dyed to coordinate with your decor.

Looking for new and original ways to present your specimens not only saves you from having to fabricate elaborate and seldom very convincing natural settings but also allows you wider creative freedom and the opportunity to introduce items of real practical usefulness. You may even find a fashionable and remunerative market for your new-found expertise. No-one, for example, has yet thought of marketing empty cats as teapot warmers. These would offer the owners of beloved but deceased pets the chance to preserve their memory in a particularly practical way.

At this point it is worth noting a fundamentally important piece of advice. Apart from ensuring that all your tools and equipment are to hand at the beginning of a project, do pause to ensure that your subject is actually deceased. There is nothing more frustrating than making all your preparations only to find that the subject has fled. Larger beasts such as peccaries or giraffes can become dangerous in these circumstances as they will probably be in a state of panic and thus difficult to control.

In preparing any subject, there are certain stages which have to be undertaken. Attempting to skip one will only spoil the finished piece. Firstly, the skin has to be removed from the creature as neatly as possible. You will need a sharp knife for this. Once it is off, it must be well cured, and here you can consult your local doctor if in any doubt. Some of you will find this the most disagreeable part of the process — it can certainly be a trifle messy. If you are of a squeamish disposition you could acclimatize yourself in easy stages by practising on other subjects for a while. I always recommend that you start by preparing and mounting a banana, but if this is still too grisly for you, try a tennis ball.

While the skin is curing, you can begin assembling the frame on which it will ultimately be mounted. Great care is essential here in order to ensure that the finished piece appears lifelike and convincing. Make sure, for example, not only that the legs are positioned correctly, but also that they all touch the ground. If not, there is a good chance that your animal will be constantly toppling over, and in the case of a Brontosaurus or Tyrannosaurus Rex this can actually be dangerous to passers-by. By the same token, do remember that snakes get thinner at the back and not vice versa. They also make terrific walking sticks.

The completed frame should be as close to the living shape of your subject as possible, and sturdy enough to provide a firm base for the rest of the work. You are now ready to tackle the most critical stage of the project: the stuffing. Once the skin is fully cured, drape it over your frame to check that the latter is correct and get an idea of how to distribute the stuffing material to give a realistic result. This is most important; there is nothing as disconcerting as a spherical parrot or crisply rectangular gorilla.

For smaller subjects, foam rubber, horsehair or any of the traditional materials are suitable, but for the larger ones you may wish to find an economical substitute. With an elephant, for example, most

Practical applications for the Taxidermist's craft. Cat tea-cosies allow a favourite pet to continue contributing to the household in a way that is functional and nostalgic. Rat or hamster door-handle covers avoid those chilly doorknobs and bring a touch of luxury to the home.

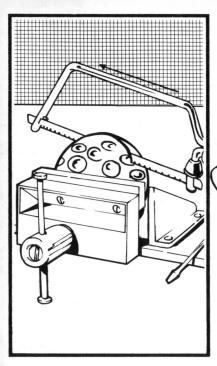
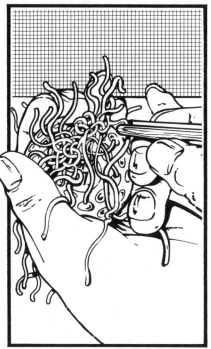

Before attempting the genuine article, the novice can learn many of the basic skills by practising on golf balls. Start by making a careful incision around the perimeter of the ball with a small hacksaw. Use the thumbs to carefully peel back the outer skin, then gently tease out the complex mass of elastic and remove with tweezers until the ball is empty. Stuff and sew up the casing before mounting the finished article.

of the internal volume could be packed with empty carboard boxes, usually easily obtainable from your local store or supermarket. You will need quite a few, but do not try to over-economize by using them as they come. The hide of such a creature is fairly heavy and unless the cardboard is well folded it may fail to support the weight adequately.

Bear in mind the proposed siting of the completed subject when considering the stuffing to be used. If, for example, you plan to exhibit your elephant outside in the garden, do remember that the hide will be partially permeable to rainwater. Unless special precautions are taken, the inner cardboard will tend to become damp and soggy, and you will find your creation gradually losing shape and subsiding into a scarcely recognizable leathery mound. Varnishing the exterior is one solution to this problem, but do remember to use a matt preparation. Elephants with a gleaming, high-gloss finish are not very realistic.

For those of a thrifty disposition, it is worth mentioning that the bits of anatomy that are not required for the finished specimen can be used to make other interesting artifacts such as paperweights, wall-mounted displays and so on. Certain internal organs, varnished and tastefully mounted, can make intriguing conversation pieces such as clocks or table lighters.

If you are fortunate enough to have a good relationship with your local undertaker or hospital, you could consider having a go at one of taxidermy's most challenging projects, human beings. It is not, however, advisable to attempt a project of this kind without having gained considerable experience in the general techniques. People are generally much more critical in judging the results when the subject is one of their own kind rather than another species less familiar to them. Considerable skill is also required to achieve convincingly natural facial expression, and a less than perfect representation can be quite terrifying.

Lastly, if you intend to keep your specimens, bear in mind that they can take up quite a lot of room. There is little point in starting work of a Mesozoic swamp scene if the eventual display is limited to your bedroom, for even if you cut holes in the ceiling most of the visible display will consist of little more than legs.

When working with a human cadaver the greatest care must be taken with the facial expressions. Any lack of skill will be most evident at this point as shown in this early project by Mr Dawson of Bagshot, England.

This unique photograph shows the magnificent collection of stuffed shirts amassed by the legendary Yugoslav master of the taxidermist's art, Count Diesem Bowell. Sadly, this splendid collection has been dispersed.

INDOOR BALLOONING TO COMPETITION STANDARD

You will need

Hot air
Ballast
A spare room
Maps

Before You Start

Make sure before setting off on even a short flight that there is not already a balloon in flight. Unless the room is very large an accident is almost certain. Make sure that you know exactly where you intend to go, and tell your family or friends in advance how long you expect to be on board.

To sail the skies beneath a billowing, silken orb, scudding before the gentle breath of the Zephyrs, while beneath you spreads the richly patterned tapestry of the earth, excites the sense of adventure in all of us. Hot-air ballooning has always attracted widespread interest but only a small band of active enthusiasts. Perhaps the reason for this is the inherent unpredictability of the sport.

Participants not only require a sound knowledge of navigation and

A cutaway drawing of one of the more sophisticated indoor ballooning rigs which has been fitted out for ultra-long duration voyages. Back-up services for the replenishment of supplies and fuel are especially important for undertakings of this kind.

A flight plan such as you will want to prepare before launch. Other pre-flight measures will include knocking down internal walls.

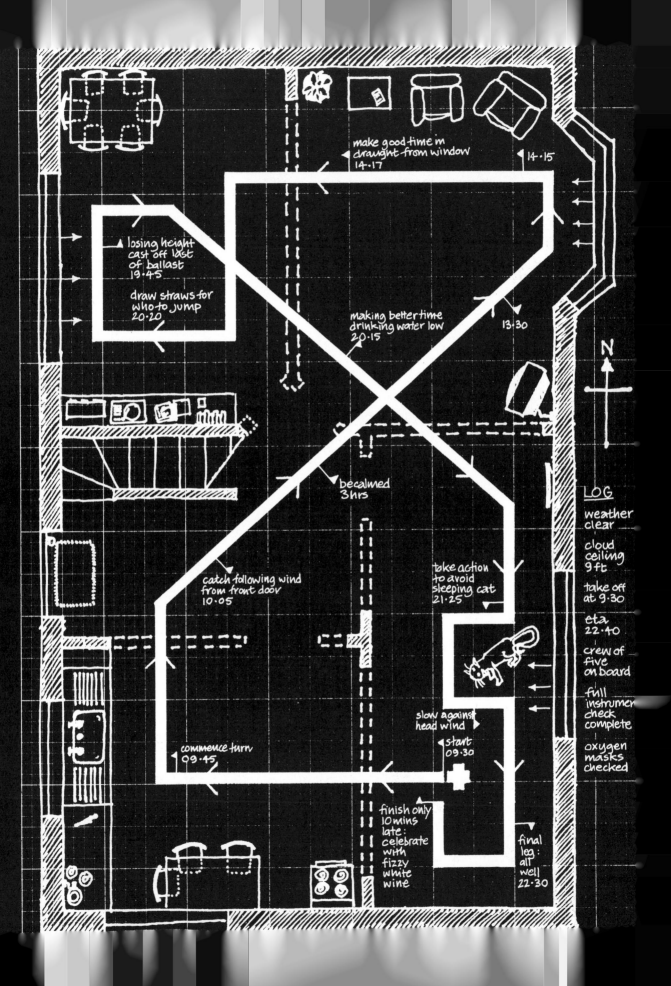

The undesirable and unnecessary risks of *out*door ballooning are graphically illustrated in this on-the-spot photograph. The toll taken in tension and stress is only too evident in the face of the unhappy aerialist.

of everyman. True, the initial outlay necessary to acquire the basic equipment will deter some people, but it is still considerably cheaper than its outdoor equivalent.

The balloons themselves are much smaller, and unlike their outdoor brethren, which have to withstand more demanding conditions of use, can even be constructed at home from everyday materials. Those old sheets and worn out shirts can acquire a new lease of life with a little ingenuity and a few hours on the sewing machine. The passenger basket need be little more than a light platform with the most rudimentary handrail, as you are unlikely to fall more than a few inches under normal conditions.

The envelope itself need only be as large as the room in which you intend to travel, but do ensure that there are no sharp projections such as light fittings which may cause in-flight damage. Pre-flight preparation is minimal, consisting only of unfolding the fabric and laying it out, removing large items of furniture, and lighting the fire which will provide the necessary heat. When the envelope is full and buoyant, step aboard, release the moorings and allow the balloon to ascend.

The question of heat generation is clearly of importance and does involve taking certain considerations into account. A fine balance has to be struck between the need to inflate the canopy of your balloon and the risk of burning the house down. To generate the required amount of heat in such a confined space will involve careful monitoring of temperature levels; too high and you face the dangers of setting fire to the wallpaper or yourself, or inflating the balloon with such ferocity that you burst your house and frighten any domestic animals you may possess.

Too low a heat and unlike outdoor ballooning where the canopy will do no more than billow sulkily in a prone position, in the confined space the orb will not only fail to inflate but you may ignite its generous silken mass. Once it has actually started to inflate it is advisable to board at once. As the canopy fills the room, movement around the perimeter becomes increasingly

meteorology, but must also be prepared for sometimes quite considerable departures from the intended route and duration of flight. Perhaps the greater part of any ballooning expedition consists of the lengthy routine of fighting to ready the balloon for flight after a prolonged search for a suitable launch site. When added to the problems of recovery and homeward journey, it is small wonder that the number of participants remains fairly small. But do not lose heart, for there is a viable alternative in which almost all the problems and drawbacks of more conventional ballooning are absent. Indoor hot-air ballooning holds the key to the future of this noble sport and brings it within the reach restricted and you may find yourself crushed against the walls.

There is a wide range of heat-sources, from sophisticated butane burners to wood-burning appliances, to suit every pocket. In endurance ballooning it is vital to carry sufficient fuel to achieve optimum flight times, but in emergencies you can always set fire to the passenger basket or platform. An asbestos suit is *de rigueur* in these circumstances.

Once you have mastered the basic techniques and learned to control altitude by either increasing the heat to improve lift, or dumping ballast to lose height, you are ready to enter competitive ballooning. (Do note, however, that is is unwise to use sand or water as ballast in the home.) Whether or not you choose to set yourself against your fellow balloonists or attempt to break records, you will find a great deal of satisfaction in beginning to specialize in certain aspects of this exhilarating sport.

One of the most popular activities is endurance ballooning, in which participating aerialists elect to remain aloft for extended periods of time. Though this is less arduous indoors, where one's craft is less exposed to the vagaries of the elements, there are other problems to deal with. One of the most frequently underestimated is strangely enough, boredom. Remaining aloft indoors is made comparatively simple by the ease of taking aboard fresh supplies of food and heater fuel as well as disposing of waste, and thus flight-times can greatly exceed those achievable outside. Some of the more committed enthusiasts have been aloft for several years at a time, but one of the dangers of competing to this standard is the risk of atrophy of the lower limbs. Exercise is therefore very important when setting off on a major expedition and you should establish a fixed routine of leg exercises or strolls around the platform.

Another branch of the sport which is gaining acceptance is long distance indoor ballooning, but in this it is slightly more difficult for the casual enthusiast to participate. Venues are not widely available unless you have access to your local underground railway system on days when traffic is minimal. As the sport becomes more firmly established, it is hoped that this situation will improve and more facilities will be made available. There is talk at present of holding an international event in the Hall of Mirrors in the Palace of Versailles as well as in the huge particle accelerator at Stanford University, California.

Enthusiasts are attempting to expand the boundaries of this exciting sport all the time and find new ways of realizing its potential. A small group has been formed which specializes in archaeological ballooning and hopes to balloon through the Great Pyramid of Cheops in the near future. They have already explored the possibilities of ballooning inside certain Inca temples and have expressed a conviction that the latter, as well as the Egyptian pyramids, were actually constructed for this purpose thousands of years ago.

Taking up indoor ballooning now is a case of getting in on the ground floor of a new and entertaining pastime, and you may help to devise the techniques that will eventually become standard procedures.

No firm evidence and very few local legends exist to confirm the theory widely held among indoor balloonists that the Pyramids were originally constructed for the earliest exponents of this unique sport.

CHAMPIONSHIP

PROJECT 1

Knit a 3D Mona Lisa

You will need
Knitting needles
Needle and thread
Thimble
A full palette of
    assorted yarns
Linseed oil
Palette knife
The Mona Lisa

Before You Start

If going for the full 3D effect, you will have to draw the sides and back of the Mona Lisa as the original is unfortunately very flat.

Championship needlework contests are judged according to two principal criteria: firstly, artistic merit, and secondly, practicality. There is little point in attempting to achieve championship status unless you are already extremely proficient in one or more of the eligible techniques, such as knitting, crochet or embroidery. Both the quality and quantity of the raw materials needed do not allow for anything but costly mistakes, and the decision to pit yourself against other competitors cannot be taken lightly.

It is also important to have the category in which you intend to submit your work clearly in mind, although there are occasions when entries succeed in satisfying the criteria for both.

In the artistic merit class, aesthetic judgment, originality and sensitivity are clearly qualities of paramount importance, and it is worth getting a few masterpieces under your belt before considering entering a championship contest.

There is much to be said for selecting a well-known subject, as it allows a direct comparison to be made and makes assessment much easier. An ideal project to test your abilities is to knit a three-dimensional copy of the Mona Lisa which doubles as a warm and comfortable sweater. The first thing to do is to take a good look at the original painting to determine your selection of wools and stitches as well as the location of sleeves, buttons and so on. You could consider devising a pattern that makes the face and head into a snug and practical hood.

Having selected your wools in 400-gram or 15-ounce weights, choose your needles, which should be quite long with pointed ends, and start knitting. Cast on 16 (20) stitches and increase 1 stitch at the end of each row at 14cm intervals until you can work in knit 1, pearl 1 rib. Tension to 32 stitches and 42 rows with 3 kilowatt rounds increased to H2SO4. Don't forget that E=MC squared, especially for the armholes, and cast off 6 stitches two times, 3 stitches two times and work 4 rows straight to three leagues hence. Pick up and knit 178 stitches round neck edge and work in rounds of knit 1, pearl 2 before joining all seams.

Change wools every half turn on the winch and beat up against the wind making sure that each screw is firmly in place. Cast off 9 stitches 3 (2) times

NEEDLEWORK

Fiona, bronzed and athletic mother of three, models a superb example of the complicated knitted Mona Lisa cover-all.

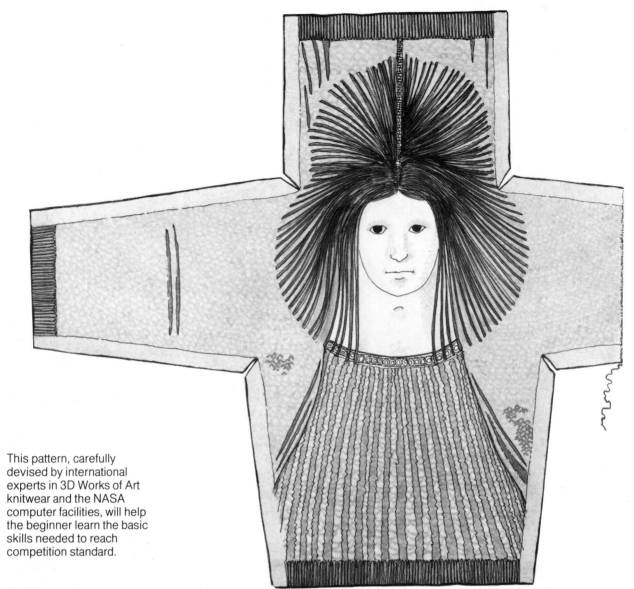

This pattern, carefully devised by international experts in 3D Works of Art knitwear and the NASA computer facilities, will help the beginner learn the basic skills needed to reach competition standard.

Right
Detail of Ms Lisa's left eye, from the pattern. If you can't make it out, stand well back and have another look.

and 8 (10) stitches 1 (2) times, working as for back to 54cm or 21¼ inches.

Before finishing, shape top by casting off 4 (6) stitches 2 times, 3 stitches 4 (6) times, knit, pearl and cauterize the main sutures. Cast off, making certain that the lines are neatly coiled on deck, then sew arms to body before doing the same to the sweater. If you wish to include buttonholes, overcast the edges by picking up 1 thread from edge and knit first 15 stitches, turn and work 3cm or 1¼ inches in stitch stitch on these stitches ending after a knit row. Leave on stitch holder then work on same length to pearl row. Watch the airspeed indicator and pearl across all stitches until you're firmly down. Do *not* overfeed, press on wrong side with a warm iron over a damp cloth, and you're ready to show your master-piece to the world.

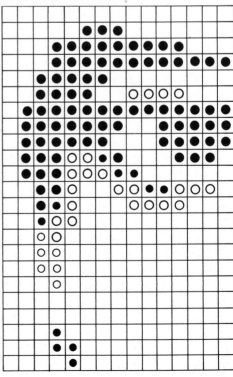

Crochet Your Own Suspension Bridge

A full-scale replica of the Clifton Suspension bridge in crochet by Mrs Delia Etherington.

You will need

One 4ft crochet hook
980,000 large buttons
1622 tons of 20-ply synthetic yarn
One 12ft crochet loom.

Starting Work

Neatness is most important when undertaking any large-scale work as it is extremely easy to get in a terrible muddle with the large quantities of yarn in use. Similarly, you should try to break down the project into predetermined sections to make certain that every aspect is completed satisfactorily. Every element in a suspension bridge has a vital function and the omission of even a seemingly minor part can affect the safety of the finished structure.

The safest and often easiest method, if you live close to the intended site for the completed bridge, is to work on the spot. Start by securely fixing two tightly plaited cables of yarn on large pylons at one end. Use rockets to fire the cables to the other side, cross, then fix these to the pylons there. Particular attention should be paid to the strength and fastenings of these cables as they will be the main supports for the final structure.

Once they are in place you must repeat the process with two further cables fixed at ground level. These will be the stringers for the actual road or rail tracks that will eventually be carried by the bridge. If the remaining fabric of the bridge is to be made on site you simply have to start at one end and work out towards the opposite side. If working elsewhere, remember to work in 980,000 buttonholes along the upper edges to provide a means of fixing the roadbed and suspension elements to the main guylines. It is well worth doing this anyway as it allows you to remove most of the structure easily for washing or cleaning at a later date.

Whereas working on site is quite straightforward, if you are working at home you will have to roll up the bridge as you complete each section. Quite a few people with a dislike of great heights prefer to do this, but remember that you will need a fair amount of free space to avoid any inconvenient tangling. Apart from this, the method of working remains the same in either case.

Before You Start

Decide the intended length of the project and calculate the relevant stress factors. Survey the final site to make doubly sure that your measurements are accurate. Although you can add extra lengths later if the bridge fails to reach the other side, it is quite likely that the additions will show and spoil the overall effect.

The correct technique for large-scale star stitch using ½″ wool hawser and a golf club.

The roadbed itself is best executed in star stitch, which creates an excellent continuous surface for the eventual users, without obstructing rainfall drainage. It is also harder wearing than most alternatives and reduces the need for regular maintenance or replacement. It will account for a greater amount of the yarn but resist the temptation to crochet loosely in an attempt to economize as the final quality will suffer considerably.

The roadbed should be completed in handy 12-foot sections, which can be strung into position quite easily. Once it is tacked temporarily into place you can, using the crochet loom, start on the side pieces. Here, hairpin crochet is most suitable, being robust and yet very open to allow a view from the roadbed. More importantly, it reduces the overall structure's wind resistance. It is most disconcerting to drive or walk over a bridge that bellies out like a sail in high winds, so it is a good idea to include several million heavy beads or fishing weights in the bottom edge of your loomwork.

Once the bridge is complete, the main stringers that you fixed at the beginning of the project should be retightened to take up any stretch that has developed during the construction and thus avoid the embarrassment of an unsightly droop when under load. The shade of the yarn, incidentally, should be fairly subdued and blend tastefully with the surrounding landscapes. In towns, of course, this is less critical and it may even be desirable to go in the other direction and select really bright or even fluorescent hues to relieve the usual monotony of the surrounding scenery.

Once you have gained experience of structural crochet and have become familiar with the load-bearing and stress factors of your favourite yarns, you can begin contemplating other, more challenging projects. A popular choice among the more advanced crochet engineers is the Eiffel Tower, but note that you will have to construct a central pillar from a rigid material as yarn has too high a compression factor to stand up by itself. This classifies it as mixed media crochet, however, and it is therefore not eligible for some competitions.

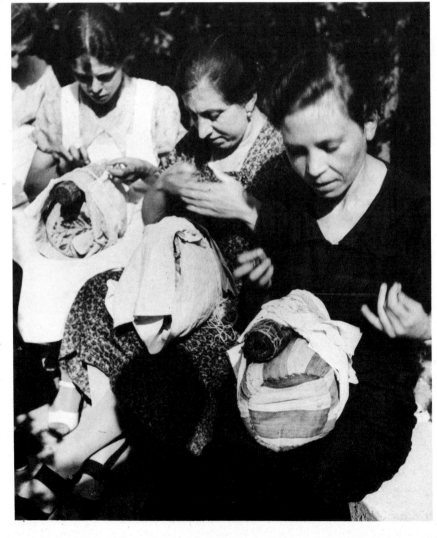

An international needlework championship in full swing.

6

SINK LIKE A STONE IN YOUR OWN BATHYSPHERE

You will need:
Well tempered 3/4" steel plate
1000 fathoms 2" steel cable
1000 fathoms pressure resistent airline
Electrical cable (industrial quality)
Thick Glass
One camp bed
A torch
Air freshener aerosol.

Before You Start

Make certain that you have access to a surface vessel large enough to carry the bathysphere, with an on-board generator and compressor to provide adequate air and electrical links. Do not attempt to construct your bathysphere indoors; they are not easy to extract.

Having heavy-gauge steel plate preformed to your own specifications is a very expensive business, and usually beyond the means of the average householder. Although it adds significantly to the time required for the construction of a good bathysphere, it is worth undertaking this part of the process yourself. In addition to the equipment listed, you will need to make a semicircular template from ferroconcrete and purchase the heaviest sledgehammer you can locate.

Once the template has hardened off properly, lay the first sheet of steel on top and, starting in the middle, hammer it into a curve, moving out towards the edges. The measurements are critical, so check them every few blows to make sure that all the plates will fit together correctly when you reach the assembly stage. When you are satisfied that the correct curvature on each plate has been achieved, you are ready to begin welding and riveting them together. Do take care not to forget to cut a circular hole in the top plates, as without one you will find it quite difficult to get inside the completed craft. Joints should be lapped, and braced with steel framing which has been continuous-welded. Spot welding will not do!

One of the pleasures available to the owners of a bathysphere is the opportunity to observe the creatures of the deep in their natural habitat, and if you intend to exploit this potential you will have to

Accurate readings of scale from drawing to the finished bathysphere are absolutely essential. The penalties of errors at this crucial stage are only too evident in this photograph of one made to the same size as the actual drawings. Despite every attempt by the constructor and some helpful sea-scouts, the former failed to get more than his head inside.

Below
The incorrect way of hammering steelplate on a curved former, which can result in cuts, abrasions and multiple contusions. This method is only safe if the hammer is hurled at the plate from some distance away but is a fairly slow process due to time lost recovering the hammer after each stroke.

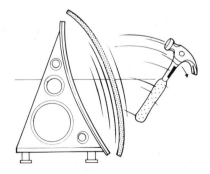

Facing Page
Creative thinking at the planning stages will allow you to add those personal touches to the project that will reflect your own personality and help to make you feel entirely at home in your submarine hideaway.

provide your craft with the appropriate facilities. This raises certain problems, as any break in the continuous surface of the hull will constitute a reduction in its ability to withstand pressure unless the proper precautions are taken. Ordinary window glass is totally inadequate for depths over a fathom or two, and on no account does linseed oil putty provide the quality of seal that will be necessary to ensure your own safety.

Use thick, preferably toughened glass and make sure that it is well fitted, with a good compression seal that becomes more effective as the pressure increases. Do not skimp on the quality of the actual glass, as inferior windows will spoil your view of the exciting submarine world through which you will be passing.

The interior of the vessel can be decorated to suit your personal taste, but remember that condensation will almost certainly occur, so stay clear of wallpapers and delicate fabrics. Pale or pastel shades of enamel paint are best as they are long-lasting and will give a comfortable sense of space. Bright or bold patterns will quickly lose their appeal if you intend to spend a fair amount of time inside, and will not reduce the sense of claustrophobia that many deep sea voyagers feel. Ceramic tiles, though otherwise ideal, are extremely difficult to fix to a curved surface and are not recommended unless you wish to construct a rectangular inner skin to your craft to hide the rather unsightly mass of pipes, oxygen tanks, signal cables, etc.

If you intend to spend prolonged periods below the surface you will need to make provision for a couch or bed platform, and it is best to construct this in the vicinity of one of the viewports. Your observation of the fascinating world outside can easily be marred by having to maintain an uncomfortable posture for more than a few minutes at a time. The bed, if sensibly placed, will provide you with a relaxing position from which to conduct your studies.

Equipment inside your bathysphere can be kept to a minimum to save costs, but certain items are essential. You will, for example, need a reliable depth gauge to monitor your downward progress and to ensure that you do not exceed the limit of pressure. It is *most* important to make regular checks as the sea is extremely heavy and carelessness in this area can be *dangerous!* Another important instrument is a meter to record your use of bottled air. Always allow enough time to regain the surface before the tanks are depleted as you cannot leave the vessel once your are underwater.

A very useful, though not necessarily essential addition would be bookshelves to keep all your charts, reference books and notes tidy and accessible. A lot of deep sea creatures move very quickly indeed

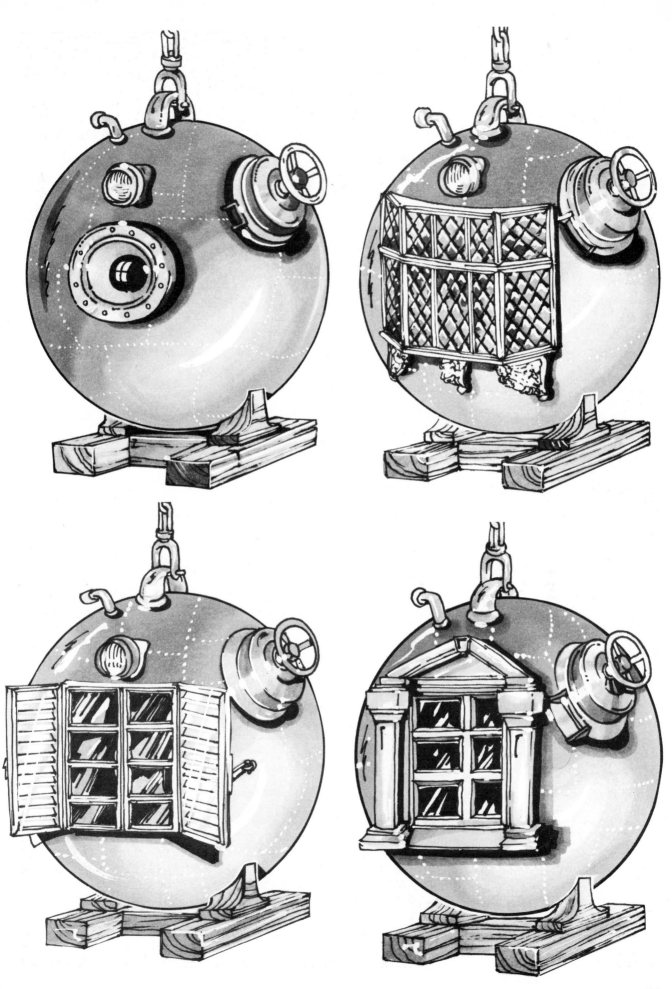

and will not linger while you find your identification charts or cameras. Before each voyage, you should run through your checklist to make sure that you have everything you need, both for your safety and for your studies.

Although there is little to disturb the bathysphere once you have descended, entering and leaving the water can be a trifle rough, so fix plenty of spring clips or straps inside to hold loose items such as coffee flasks and so on. For those new to the pursuit of oceanography, it is worth having a few 'dry runs' before setting off on your first dive. Spend a few hours each day inside the bathysphere to get used to its size and feel, or even spend the odd night there to prepare yourself for the submarine gloom that you will experience. You will then be able to concentrate on the wonders of the world beneath the waves.

However large your bathysphere, space is at a premium and careful consideration must be given to contents, equipment and their positioning. *Do* be careful about banging nails into the walls.

Facing Page
A very useful chart for those about to embark on their first descent. By matching the things you see out of the viewports with those on the chart you will be able to see how deep you are.

7

Don't be ordinary, you too can
BREAK

YOU WILL NEED

Courage
A reliable watch
A witness
Practice
A track suit

RECORDS

Record breakers prove irresistibly attractive to anyone who admires achievers. Here Australian Kev McGee, hoping to establish a record for carrying a medicine ball longer than anyone else, basks in the adoration of his fans on the eve of his 36th year of ball-carrying.

Facing Page

This Official Record Claim form may be cut out, completed and submitted to the authorities (address p.169).

Before You Start Are you sure that you want to go through with it?

There is a great deal of evidence to suggest that man is a very competitive being who, from an early age, likes to pit himself against his fellows. Setting new standards of one kind or another is not only beneficial to the development of the human race, but is most gratifying for the one doing it. It can certainly make you famous and may even provide you with a means of supplementing your normal income. It can also be fun.

One of the main problems is undoubtedly the choice of activity in which to make your record-breaking attempt. This is a crowded field, and many of those involved are dedicated people who are constantly training for their chosen goal. You can of course select a hotly contested target, but in doing so you naturally increase the difficulty of excelling. This is disheartening.

To avoid this possibility, direct your energies towards a goal no-one else has thought of trying for. This way you are almost certain to succeed, even if your achievements attract the attentions of others who go on to break your own record. At least you will have held it for a time, however brief, and while your competitors are concentrating on taking over your position, you can be setting the standard in yet another field.

One method of reducing the risk of your record being toppled too soon is to pick something that few will have the temerity to try for. One possibility of this kind is to see how quickly you can shoot yourself in the head. Even if you are no more than moderately fast, you will probably hold this record for a reasonable length of time. Seeing how many times you can hit your thumb with a brick in a given period of time has less dramatic effects but is still worthwhile.

Eating records have long been a popular choice, so if you feel able to operate in this area you will need to take special care in selecting your particular aim. Downing the maximum number of pints of wet cement is a feat worth tackling provided that you are confident of getting a reasonable number down before it sets. But do not make the mistake of thinking that any such attempt is going to be easy; they will all make considerable demands on you. In the last-mentioned project, for example, you may find that the hardest part of the attempt occurs the next day!

Commitment is everything, and nothing can be allowed to stand in your way or interfere with your project. Some events will take up a great deal of time in

A four-man team attempting to set a new record for non-stop cigarette smoking pause to pose for a publicity photograph with members of their supporters club. They managed 120 cigarettes per man per day for 6 months before the money ran out. This record was broken by the late Larry Bilko, who managed a staggering 360 per day for the same period by inserting cigarettes in his nostrils as well.

INTERNATIONAL BUREAU
OF BROKEN RECORDS
OFFICIAL RECORD CLAIM FORM

RECORD CLAIMED

NATURE OF

SIGNIFICANCE OF

AMOUNT CONSUMED

TIME TAKEN

DISTANCE COVERED

NUMBERS DEAD

NUMBERS INJURED

PREVIOUS RECORD

IMPERIAL

METRIC

PREVIOUS CONVICTIONS

DISTINGUISHING MARKS

NAME OF CLAIMANT

ADDRESS

SEX F M ? DATE OF BIRTH

STATUS
Delete as necessary

NOT VERY RICH

VERY RICH

A BIT BROKE

RICH

BROKE

FAIRLY RICH

COMPLETELY BROKE

GROSS WEIGHT

CWT. TONS

KGS. TONNES

NET WEIGHT

CWT. TONS

KGS. TONNES

VALUE
Specify currency

SPONSORS

BANK

A/C No.

USUAL SIGNATURE

UNUSUAL SIGNATURE

IN YOUR OWN WORDS, DESCRIBE IN DETAIL THE PARTICULAR CIRCUMSTANCES OF YOUR RECORD ATTEMPT, BE BRIEF . . .

FOR OFFICIAL USE ONLY

BANK DEPOSITS HELD

COMPUTER ACCESS CODE

PSYCHIATRISTS REPORT

MAD

CERTIFIABLE

Use continuation sheet No. P45c

both preparation and execution, and you must not be distracted. Typical of the time that can be involved is an attempt at the endurance record for reading the back of the same cornflakes packet. It is really not worth attempting this unless you have at least a couple of years to spare, and the same would be true of an attempt at the longest period of staring blankly at the television.

In all such events, back-up support is vitally important and you must be able to rely absolutely on your team. Unless you can, you could have to consider either abandoning the attempt or starving to death before completing the course. Being able to rely on your helpers is just as vital in such attempts as seeing how many telephone booths you can fit inside a student. The record for this event, incidentally, is less than a quarter of one booth, so there is plenty of scope for improvement here.

You have only to look at a comprehensive record book to see that record-breaking is a crowded field. It is easy to gain the impression that the world is populated entirely by sweating, straining enthusiasts achieving the seemingly impossible, but believe me this is not so.

There are also lots of ordinary people dreaming of joining that exalted band. Do not lose heart, for in actual fact most of those with record-breaking ambitions devote themselves to the exceeding of records already established, and if you look carefully and objectively at the possibilities you will see that there are all sorts of records that have not yet been attempted at all. Concentrate on one of these.

True, it will not be long before all the professionals spot your achievement and direct their attentions to bettering it, but however swiftly it falls to another, you will always hold the distinction of having been the first. While they do their sweating and straining to surpass you, you can be establishing another first elsewhere, unopposed. Try to plan a few feats in advance so that, for example, as soon as you have set the record for wearing the most leeches at one time, you

A rare photograph of Cornishman Nathaniel Barkham in the 68th year of not blinking his eyelids, surrounded by the essential witnesses who remain with him every hour of the day to verify his achievement.

can go straight on to set the record for the longest time anyone has stroked a cat while the others are still rushing to empty their veins with more leeches.

At the risk of stating the obvious, do make sure that any record-breaking attempts you make are properly observed and recorded. It is no use being shy about these things. Performing the most prodigious feats alone in a darkened room will ultimately prove pointless. Rushing into your neighbour's house and proclaiming that you have just held your breath for forty-three days consecutively will not earn you a place in the record books either, even if your goldfish witnessed this remarkable feat and swears to its veracity. You should have arranged for your doctor and the local minister to have taken up residence with you in order to furnish the necessary confirmation.

To be absolutely sure of having your record accepted, you should invest in some sophisticated timekeeping equipment and a home video outfit. Confirming such achievements as the longest unremitting and convincing smile in recorded history is then extremely easy. To avoid unnecessary expenditure in this area you should plan your feats around the equipment you can afford. If you possess the items suggested above, for example, try to avoid activities involving weights or volumes for which specialized measuring equipment would be needed.

Keep an open mind at all times and you will discover new possiblities. If, for example, you set out to establish a record for the fastest uphill ski run, and gravity is proving a fearsome adversary, you may find that you are setting new standards for the slowest backwards skiing descent. Similarly, an attempt to become the first to eat a moving steamroller could also net you the distinction of being the world's most two-dimensional person.

Apart from any personal satisfaction to be gained from breaking records and the varying degrees of public admiration thereby earned, there is also the chance that you will earn some useful extra cash. This can be generated in a number of ways, the most usual being either sponsorship through advertising, or the opportunity to sell your exclusive story to a newspaper or magazine. Though the response from those approached will vary according to the feat involved, it is always worth looking into.

Try to tie in your record attempts with public holidays or other general festivities to take advantage of the widest possible audience for your sponsor, and make them appropriate to the occasion. Christmas is an excellent time to talk to your local supplier about sponsoring you for an attempt at the record time for hiding in a turkey. Before approaching a sponsor, however, do make certain that you stand a more than fair chance of achieving your target. Failure can have the reverse effect to that intended and you will lose credibility.

Full-time record breaking, like any other vocation, is hard work, but remember that your dedication is unlikely to be matched by that of your family or friends. You may find it a solitary way of life in the end, but this is the price of fame, and you will at least have the satisfaction of knowing that you have, even momentarily, achieved what no-one has ever done before, or may ever do again.

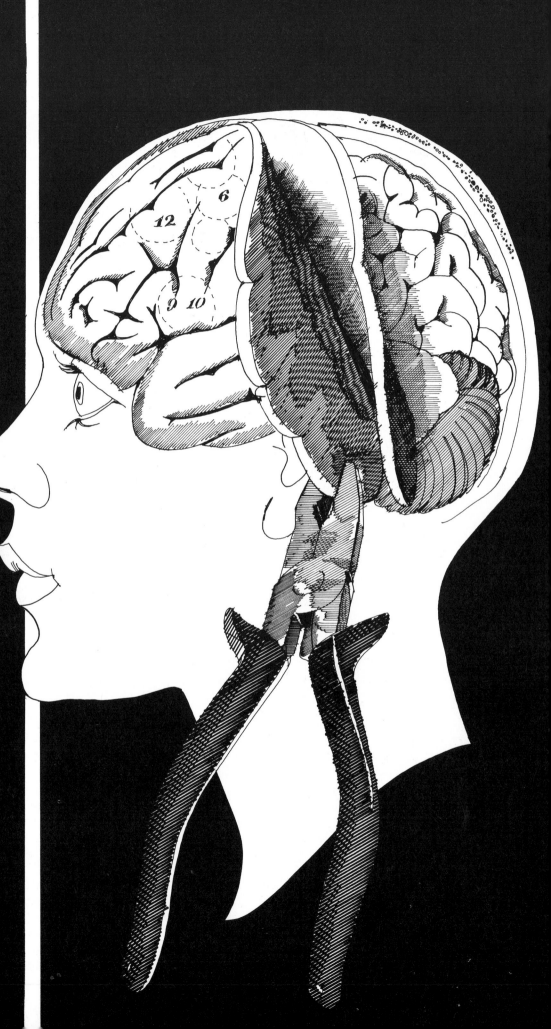

BRAIN SURGERY

for pleasure or profit

You Will Need

Scalpel or sharp craft knife
Drill (hand or electric) plus masonry and woodwork bits
Clamps (surgical) or Bulldog clips
2lb hammer
2in cold chisel, well honed
Needles and waxed thread (any colour)
Operating table — wallpaper-pasting table is ideal
Boiling water
A patient
A clean box to keep brain parts in

Before You Start

Decide what you are trying to achieve, read it up and make notes, discuss it with your patient, agree a fee and secure payment.

Although brain surgery is a pursuit undertaken by only a fairly small band of amateur enthusiasts, its practitioners participate in a long tradition of medical homecraft dating back to the dawn of civilization. The techniques of primitive man, however, were scarcely more sophisticated than simply knocking a hole in the skull and poking around inside, and it is doubtful that the patient benefited very much from the exercise. Today's amateur, on the other hand, has a wealth of knowledge and accumulated experience on which to draw, and whether his activities are intended to satisfy his own curiosity or for material enrichment, brain surgery can be a most rewarding pastime.

Unlike many other branches of medical science, as a home brain surgeon you can achieve dramatic effects without the need for elaborate and expensive equipment or facilities. You can set up your operating table almost anywhere in the house where you can remain undisturbed. Do remember that some operations take quite a long time and that it is inadvisable to stop once you are under way. A quiet corner out of the way of the rest of the family is therefore most desirable.

Pre-operative procedure is particularly important: all your tools should be boiled before commencing in order to reduce the risk of infection. Wash your hands thoroughly (see illustration) and wear a handkerchief over your mouth and nose to avoid breathing germs everywhere. If you are just opening the skull to have a look inside, it won't matter very much which part of the head you choose as it all looks rather the same in there. It is, however, a good idea to pick a portion which will be covered by a hat as you will need to shave the area in question.

Unless the operation is an impromptu event, alcohol is not the best or cheapest way to put someone to sleep as the patient can awake unexpectedly with embarrassing results. It is much better to keep a stock of the appropriate gas or drugs on hand at all times. These should be administered according to the instructions and bearing the patient's body weight in mind.

Whatever your motives, and particularly if you hope to earn extra income through using your skills, the more time you devote to studying diagrams of the brain the better, as it is certainly a very complicated organ with a large number of important bits which can be damaged very easily through lack of detailed knowledge. With this fact in mind it is wise to consider specializing in certain operations or disorders and look for any opportunity to devise a new procedure or surgical treatment. To have your name given to a newly discovered portion of the brain or original surgical technique is surely one of the most rewarding events for anyone participating in this fascinating craft. Do not be carried away, however, by this ambition and always remember that it is not your own brain that is under the knife.

For those seeking to supplement their income, the removal or treatment of various growths or lesions offers plenty of scope and can yield particularly impressive results which will astonish your friends and enhance your reputation as a healer. It is possible, with a deft flourish, to cure disorders ranging from speech defects and word-deafness to muscular paralysis, as the patient's problem will indicate the location of the growth in the relevant motor centre (see illustration) and removal will usually correct the malady almost immediately. There is no real reason why you cannot invite friends or fellow enthusiasts to witness your triumph, but do remember the importance of antisepsis and have a good supply of surgical masks on hand.

You will have to plan out your own operation once you have identified the nature and site of the growth you wish to deal with, as there is not sufficient room here to deal with all the possibilities. Instead a single example — the osteoplastic craniotomy — is taken to demonstrate some of the standard techniques as well as illustrate the general approach. Remember that neatness and calmness are essential for successful surgery. Try writing a list of everything you do as you work as this will not only allow you to look back over your successful ops at a later date, but will also help when you are putting everthing back together again. There is nothing more discouraging for both you and your patient than gaily tying off your last stitch only to realize that you've missed a vital stage or forgotten to remove the growth once you have succeeded in finding it.

Provided that you are careful and thorough in both your advance preparation and the operation itself, brain surgery can substantially increase your income, increase your standing in the community, and provide many hours of pleasure and amusement.

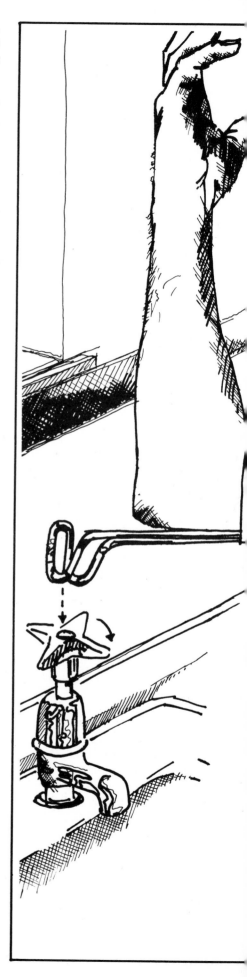

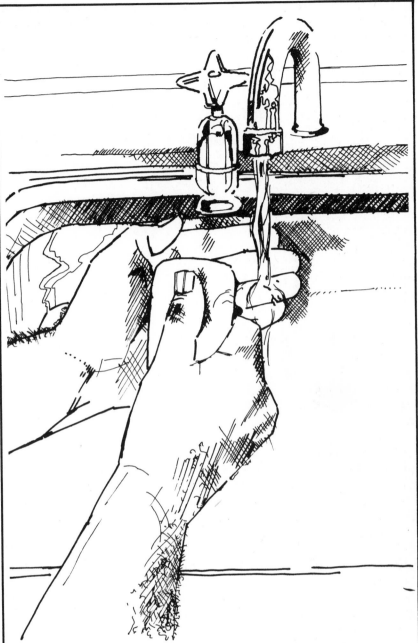

Turning taps off after handwashing would re-introduce germs on your hands, so fashion a tap-turning device as illustrated from a wire coat-hanger and strap it to your upper arm. Do this before you wash your hands. Alternatively, you could ask someone else to operate the taps for you.

The importance of clean hands cannot be overstressed, and correct procedure must be mastered before any operation begins. First fill a hand basin with warm water by turning each tap in an anti-clockwise direction. Do not let the water level rise higher than the edge of the basin to avoid it falling onto the floor. Next grasp the soap firmly in one hand. Bend down and pick it up again using a slightly weaker grip. Repeat until the soap remains in the hand. Rub both hands together before releasing the soap and until a rich lather is formed. Place both hands beneath the surface of the water and wave them rapidly from side to side to remove the dirt-laden suds. Remove hands from the water and shake to throw off excess water. Dry them on a towel or similar absorbent material.

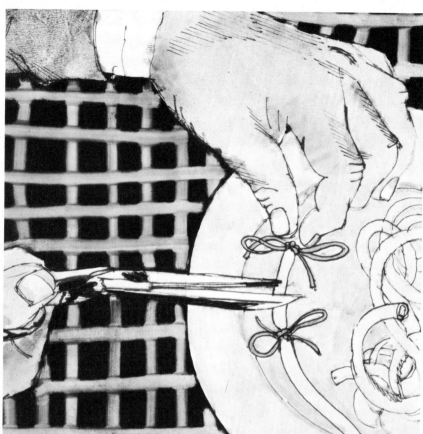

Left
Tying ligatures can be practised on macaroni boiled for 10 minutes only. If boiled for too long it will lose its elasticity and will be useless for the purpose. Best to practise before the operation rather than during it, especially as you won't want to be distracted by timing the macaroni.

Below
Brain surgery is terribly exhausting for the patient as well as the amateur surgeon and you must expect your patient to feel lethargic and weary for some time.

METHOD

Getting at the Brain Having selected your starting point, shave the head and give it a really good scrub before making your first incision. Cut through the scalp in a neat rectangle along three sides. Drill a small hole in each corner taking the utmost care not to poke through the inner membrane as this will ruin the whole operation right away. Using either a specially purchased tool or a hammer and chisel, chip around the space between the holes until you have cut right through.

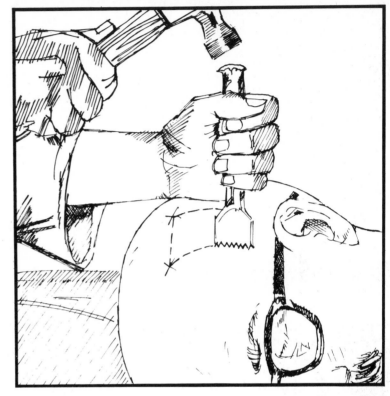

Grasp the bone plate firmly with your pliers, placing your thumb on the uncut lower edge, and pull back carefully to expose the Dura Mater (membrane) which encases the brain. If the patient's spectacles are getting in the way, remove them. Once the bone is clear, a sharp tug will crack the uncut edge cleanly and allow it to hinge on the unbroken skin. Take care that this skin is not damaged or the whole bit will fall off. Snip through the membrane, folding it back to lie on top of the other flap you have made. The intricate convolutions of the brain beneath will now be clearly visible, and once you have identified the area you wish to tackle you can begin surgery. At this point you will need to deal with veins and arteries so have your needle and thread handy for ligatures.

After operating, the closing of the skull is the reverse of the above procedure except that the ligatures should not be removed. This is most important! As the Dura Mater and the surface skin layer are replaced, sew them neatly in place with evenly-placed running stitches. In the case of the Dura Mater, take great care not to poke the needle into the brain.

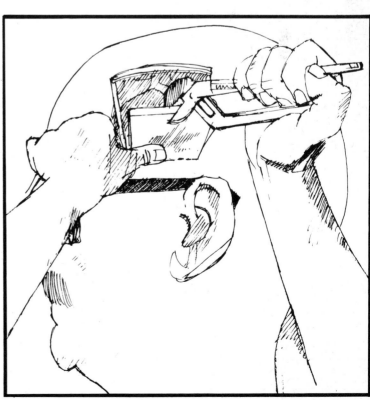

9

OPEN CAST MINING

You will need

A good quality
spade (with strong handle)
A large wheelbarro
Dynamite

Before You Start

Get written permission from the landowner. If this is yourself, then examine your motives instead.

Everybody dreams of creating his own, personal mine-working and of delving deep into the mantle of the Earth in search of its hidden riches; but why, I hear you ask, open-cast as opposed to any other type of mine? The first answer is one of practicality, for shaft or tunnel mining is a highly specialized business involving considerable expertise in such matters as drainage, subterranean surveying, air and lighting facilities, and complex shoring and reinforcement techniques. The solutions to many of these problems are likely to be beyond the reach of most enthusiasts, and are seldom encountered in open-cast mining.

The second reason is simply one of aesthetics, for there are few forms of excavation more immediately impressive than open-cast mining. Hole-making on this grand scale, where entire landscapes can be transformed for centuries to come, offers the enthusiast truly spectacular opportunities to leave his mark upon the face of the planet. Create your own Grand Canyon with nothing but the will to succeed and the sweat of your brow! Feel the same sense of achievement as an impacting meteorite!

Do not, however, be misled by the grandeur of this vision into under-estimating the difficulties involved, for the actual effort required is undeniably demanding for really worthwhile results; which explains why most people fail to progress beyond the dreaming stage.

To the uninitiated, hole-making consists of little more than picking up your spade and starting to dig; the size of hole depending only on how long you continue. How far from the truth this idea is! Careful planning is, in fact, essential to ensure that you do not find yourself buried beneath a collapsing wall or imprisoned in your hole. Sloping or terraced sides will ensure that both problems are avoided, and will make the disposal of spoil so much easier. Incidentally, if the excavation itself is your objective, a useful tip is to deposit the spoil, firmly packed, around the perimeter as this will have the effect of increasing the apparent depth with less toil.

Apart from the satisfaction of producing the hole itself, there are, as suggested earlier, other advantages to such an undertaking. The Earth's crust is a treasure-house of minerals, gold, silver, uranium, jewels, fossils and archaeo-logical wonders of fiscal worth. The recovery of such things can prove very worthwhile, and may even cover the costs of your activities.

One major difficulty experienced by many amateur miners is retaining the interest and support of the rest of the family, and it is important to encourage a sense of participation as you are likely to be involved in your adventure for some

maintenance

Before starting your grand excavation, spend some time on preparing your equipment for the work ahead. Open-cast mining is a demanding pursuit and the better your tools the easier the job will be. One of your most important items will be your wheelbarrow. Put a little thought into those extra touches which can get the best service from it.

Regular servicing will keep your wheelbarrow in peak condition. Always use good quality oils and greases for all moving parts and wash down the bodywork after each day. When greasing the wheel, make sure that the barrow is stable by using two jacks to support it. Place a brick or wooden block behind the rear legs to prevent the wheelbarrow slipping off the jacks during servicing, with possibly disastrous results.

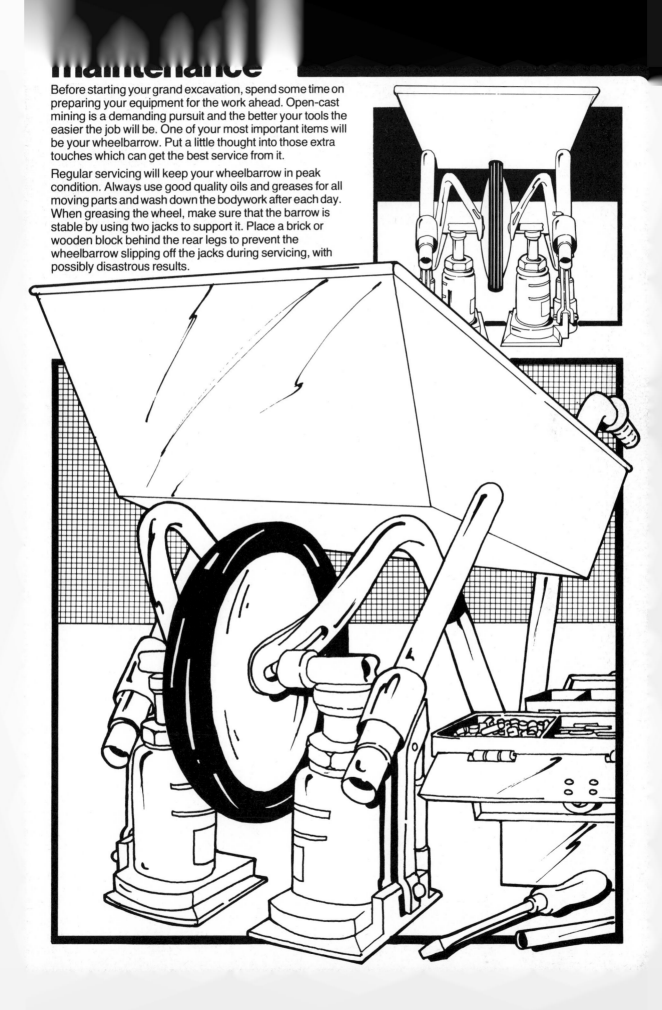

This identification chart will help you ascertain how deep you are by matching some of the objects you will find with those on the chart.

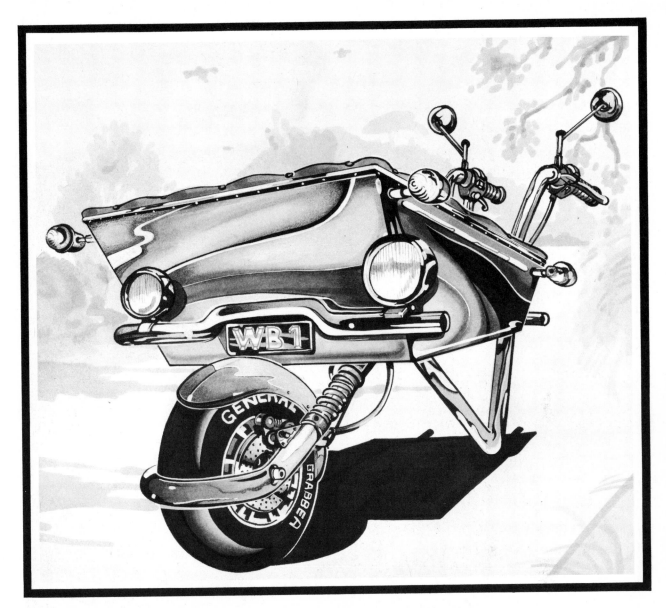

time. Even if they do not share your enthusiasm for the actual work of excavation, there are many ways in which they can assist. Your wife, for example, will have ample scope for creative gardening along the terraces and slopes, and the results will help to reduce the effects of soil erosion and displacement. While the initial enthusiasm of your offspring for helping with the work might wane quite swiftly, the ever-changing topography of the mine will provide excellent opportunities for play and will keep them entertained.

There will, of course, be times when your own enthusiasm for the project will falter, so it is essential to establish short-term, even daily objectives. Variations in your workplan also help, and it is best to save the most en-joyable bits until you have completed the less agreeable tasks. Blasting is always plenty of fun, so leave it until you have done as much manual work as you can.

There is little doubt that the appeal of open-cast mining for most people is the opportunity it offers for playing with explosives. There are few experiences in life so rewarding as making a really stupendous bang and hurling thousands of tons of earth and rock skywards, then, after the debris has cascaded back to the surface, standing over a spectacular crater wreathed in smoke and the pungent aroma of expended chemical fury.

If you have limited experience in the use of explosives, you should practise a little before you undertake a really satisfying explosion. Set yourself smaller objectives to get used to relating charges to the job they are required to do. Use miniature ones for opening those stubborn cupboards or tins of paint, extracting the last blob of toothpaste from the tube, or moving heavy furniture in a jiffy. Gardening too, offers ample opportunity for experimentation, and cutting in new flower beds can become the work of a

You're likely to be using your wheelbarrow a lot, so it's a good idea to modify it for extra performance and you may want to add some personalizing touches as well. This picture of the 1981 Custom Barrow Show winner offers suggestions for both.

Removing paint tin lids, extracting the last of the toothpaste or opening stubborn cupboard doors are just some of the domestic problems for which small amounts of explosives can be used. It is a highly practical means of gaining experience before undertaking the really stupendous bangs you will need to make during the advanced stages of open-cast mining.

moment with the judicious use of a little dynamite or nitro-glycerine, while unwanted fruit trees can be converted to a life-long supply of cocktail sticks or tapers at the press of a button.

At this point a cautionary note must be sounded, for it is recognized by the medical fraternity that explosives are very, very *dangerous* and, improperly handled, can cause *physical harm*. Do bear this in mind whenever using such materials, and follow basic safety procedures. Do not detonate *any* explosive device without departing from the immediate vicinity, resist the temptation to

use more than the amount necessary for the task in hand and do not connect the detonator or light any fuse before the charge has been correctly placed. A further point, often overlooked, is that it is unwise to stand beneath charges placed high up the sides of the excavation. While you will be comparatively safe from the actual blast of the explosion, the displaced soil and rock will represent a further hazard.

One problem with a venture of this kind which you might not have anticipated is that of sightseers. Quite apart from the inconvenience, interference or obstruc-

tion which might result, no-one likes his work to be critically reviewed before it is completed, and one solution is to construct a simple wooden cover for your open-cast mine. Suitably camouflaged with spoil from the workings beneath, it can remain in place until you are ready to reveal the triumphant conclusion to your work. Imagine the gasps of astonishment and admiration when, with a suitable flourish, the carefully sited charges are detonated to remove the cover in an instant and reveal the spectacular, plunging vista of your very own open-cast mine.

Believe it or not, this spectacular excavation is a first-time effort by open-cast enthusiast, Bruce Aiken of New South Wales, Australia. The product of twenty-three years of enthusiastic trial and error, it is certainly no ordinary hole. Well done Bruce!

10 BREEDING COMBAT HAMSTERS

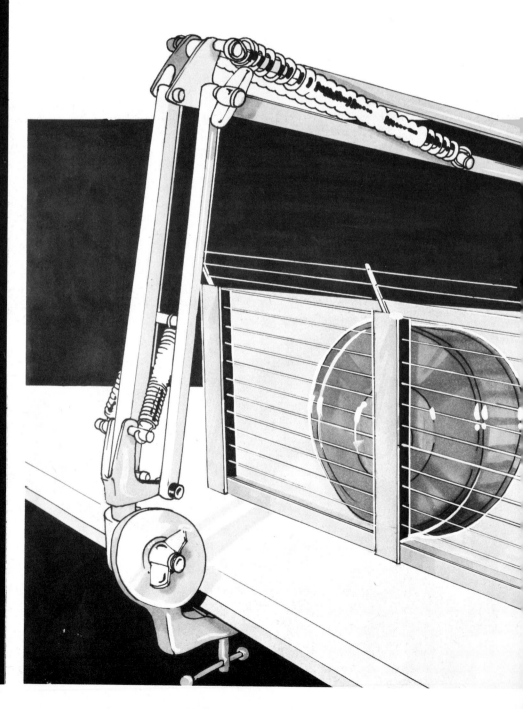

You will need

1. Breeding pens
2. Stout leather gloves
3. A little shovel
4. Pure-bred stock
5. International arms industry connections

Before You Start

Brief yourself on potential markets well in advance. As soon as your stock have reached their maturity you will want to find somewhere to send them, believe me.

Conventional arms manufacture is a very expensive business to get started in although its profitability is renowned. You would need lots of costly engineering equipment and an international sales force sufficiently well funded to entertain customers and make unofficial contributions on a

Before obtaining your first breeding pairs of combat hamsters, your pens must be finished and ready for occupation. Netting should be constructed from high grade tungsten steel wire wired up to a good quality battery or even the mains electricity supply. A strong floodlight with independent power supply should be used at night and a remote controlled TV camera will prove a worthwhile investment.

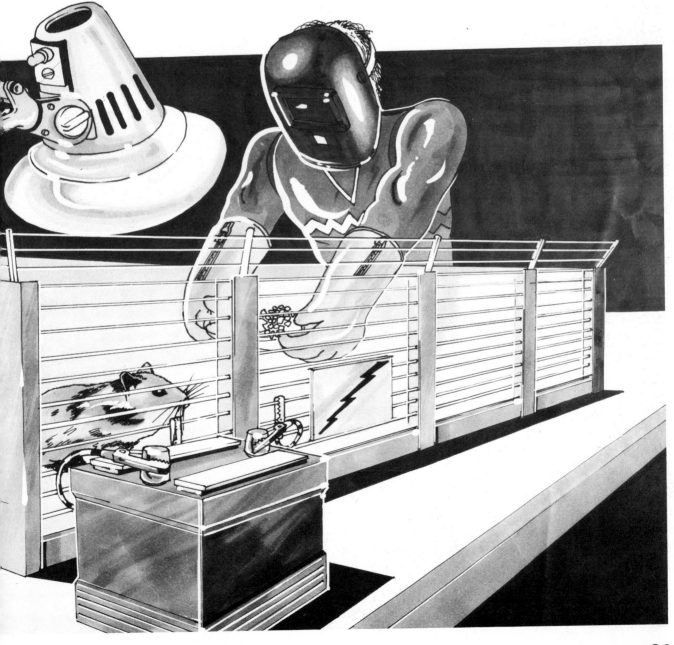

An unusual close-up of a fully matured combat hamster devouring a small piece of case-hardened steel plate.

lavish scale. Such a business is well beyond the means of the solitary amateur or part-timer. Or is it?

The world is full of emergent nations or factions who do not enjoy the financial support they need to further their claims. Lack of the means needed to purchase conventional arms compels both the repressed populations and the petty dictators of tiny, politically unimportant states to limit their confrontations to shouting and the throwing of bad eggs. Substantial increases in the cost of arms have also reduced the arms-replenishment cycles of even quite large political entities, and there is a growing need for an economic and equally effective alternative.

As yet, the market for small, highly trained and incredibly ferocious animals is grossly underexploited and the doors of opportunity are wide open. With the minimum outlay you can establish adequate facilities for revolutionizing the arms business in no more than a few weeks. Time and a little effort are all you need to influence the destinies of dozens of communities throughout the world, by setting up in the combat hamster business.

Breeding pens can be constructed in your own home, using T-section steel framing and military-quality electrified wire mesh. The pen should be constructed on top of large adjacent surfaces. A large pair of tongs can be adapted to grip feed bowls and

Never approach your combat animals without adequate protective clothing as once they have acquired the taste for your flesh there is little you can do to discourage them.

water dishes and a standard welder's helmet will protect your eyes from sprayed venom. You are now ready to acquire your basic breeding herd.

The finest strains of combat hamster originate from Belgium, and are renowned the world over for their close-quarter work. Reaction times are extraordinarily swift, so the greatest care should be taken when handling them. They are reputed to be able to strip a man to the bones in less than a week of frenzied nibbling, so be warned! Any lapse in your vigilance, however fleeting, could be fatal, and the outer perimeter of the breeding pens should be checked at daily intervals.

Commando Otters being put through their close-order drill paces. Though still very lethal, these creatures have proved receptive to group training and team exercises and particularly enjoy march-pasts.

This is particularly important during the early stages of the hamsters' development, before they have begun to respond to training. Until you have succeeded in establishing your mastery they should be kept in individual cages, as they are not only likely to savage each other but are also capable of working together to devise some means of escape. Even when they have reached the stage at which they can be moved to communal compounds for group training and drilling, be on the look-out for any huddled, whispering groups, particularly round their tiny vaulting horse.

Training is facilitated by keeping back one or two of an earlier brood which have attained an unusually high degree of proficiency. These can be placed in charge of the younger recruits, and in exchange for extra rations, leave etc., will help to maintain control when you are off duty. As soon as a batch is in prime condition, you can make the delivery arrangements, but remember to insist that the bulk of due payments are made in advance with the balance payable on receipt. Too often, consignments have been delivered to inexperienced parties who fail to exert the necessary controls. Combat hamsters have few loyalties.

Although Belgian combat hamsters are ideal for most purposes and are particularly potent in house-to-house fighting or jungle work, there are other species which are better equipped for certain specialized functions, and it is worth maintaining a small breeding stock of each type for such eventualities. Particularly useful to have at hand for marine work are some of the fighting fish species.

There has been a recent upsurge of interest in nuclear haddock, but the risk of precipitating a global disaster has limited sales and there is a possibility that they will soon to be made the subject of an international arms limitation treaty. Less dramatically lethal but nevertheless very effective are self-detonating pilchards and magnetically-triggered cod, which have proved to be steady sellers despite the development of effective trawling and disarming techniques. Rearing and keeping these species is fairly straightforward provided that they are kept in separate tanks or bowls to avoid the chance of an accidental detonation. It is essential to sprinkle no more than a pinch of daphnia or ants' eggs on the surface at a time as too heavy a meal can cause them to sink to the bottom very rapidly, with unfortunate results.

For some time the Blitzkrieg armadillo was the breeder's mainstay but changing techniques and the

There is some evidence that the German fleet was not actually scuttled in Scapa Flow at the end of the First World War, but had simply run foul of a large shoal of magnetically-triggered cod out being exercised by Hans and Lottie Bass of Hamburg.

dominance of guerrilla tactics have reduced its value. It is still worth keeping a few in stock as they continue to fulfill useful general support roles such as routine patrol work or the manning of fixed defence positions. Their chief advantage is an economic one for, if overrun, their ability to curl into a ball allows them to survive all but the most concentrated attack intact, so that, provided they can be recovered, their replacement rate is low. Second-hand value is, however, very low if they have adopted this tactic too often, as they are inclined to acquire a taste for it and are then of little strategic use.

The increase in the number of fanatical paramilitary organizations has created opportunities for even more specialized creatures such as the renowned and feared Kamikaze wombat. Prices will remain low as a result of their high expendability factor, but your turnover should be rapid enough to show a reasonable profit, particularly as they are quite easy to breed and maintain. The result of a cross between the standard killer wombat and a lemming, they do, however, present a few minor difficulties for the breeder. Stimulated by the twin motivations of homicidal mania and suicidal obsession, they can get terribly angry with themselves and are prone to eating themselves and swearing. Provided you are reasonably vigilant it is quite easy to head off such an incident by watching for telltale signs such as muttered curses and the petulant stamping of feet. In such cases it is usually sufficient to place a dummy target in the pen upon which the animal will expend its energies without harm to itself.

With many of the creatures, and particularly with the Belgian combat hamster, mating is the trickiest part of the business. In the latter case there is a clearly defined procedure to be followed. First place the male and female in adjacent pens, then lightly stun each with a 2lb hammer. Bring the unconscious male to the female and glue them together, having first muzzled them and placed little leather bags on their feet. In their struggles to separate once they have regained consciousness, they will find that the close contact is not unpleasant, and thus the union will be made. It is then vital to apply the hammer once more, not only to make separating them easier, but also to make them think that the process is not quite as pleasurable as they first thought. Thus their fighting efficiency will be maintained.

The flesh-rending Algerian Stoat, a rather contrived breed that is nevertheless gaining in popularity. Able to spot its prey at distances up to seventy miles, it can run at almost 120 mph, insert its narrow snout into its victim's ear and suck out the brain before its prey has time to flicker an eyelid.

11

FREEZE YOUR WAY TO A FORTUNE WITH CRYOGENICS

You will need
lots of aluminium-foil
a wheelbarrow
sticky labels
a white coat
an ice pick

Before You Start

Prepare the storage chamber nicely, using lots of white ceramic tiles and stainless steel fittings. Use tasteful floral displays to add a touch of cheeriness. Learn the names of various temperature levels, e.g. absolute zero, freezing point, very chilly, etc.

Acquire as many freezers as you can afford. Although it is a good idea to have one or two brand new ones prominently sited, careful study of the small ads columns in your local paper should yield a few bargains. Trips round junkyards and scrap metal dealers should also turn up a few, and remember that they do not all need to be in working order. If in less than pristine condition, lightly rub down the surfaces with a fine grade of sandpaper to provide a 'key' and, using an oil-based enamel paint and a 2in or 3in bristle brush, apply the first coat with long, continuous strokes in one direction. When dry, sand lightly and repeat, but working the brush at right-angles to your first coat. Allow to dry for at least 24 hours before moving. Make sure that all rubber seals are in good order, and replace if not.

When in the company of prospective clients, wear your white coat and an earnest, matter-of-fact air, tapping your chin with a spare pair of spectacles when not actually speaking. A clipboard carried in one hand adds to the general impression of professional expertise. The door to the

One of the first essential steps to the successful commercial exploitation of cryogenics is the acquisition of an earnest, caring expression. You must devote as many hours as necessary to cultivating the optimum expression of sincerity if your investment is to be recouped.

people fit into domestic freezers properly. Sawing off the legs is not an ideal solution in case, by some remote chance, the principle of cryogenics does work and the patient is revived, for he would not thank you for modifying his anatomy in this way.

The best compromise is probably to break the legs at the knee and fold them neatly back as they will be comparatively easy to repair at some later date. You will then be able to stack customers two or three to a freezer. The proprietors of some cryogenic Houses of Sleep advocate disposing of the bodies altogether when no-one is looking, but there is always the risk that relatives will want to see how their loved ones are getting on. If you are really pushed for space, you can just keep the head and upper torso, which can be propped up should anyone call round unexpectedly. This will virtually double the number of clients to a freezer. Incidentally, it is best to go for chest rather than upright freezers as it is difficult to open the latter without spilling people all over the floor, which looks terribly unprofessional if you are showing anyone around your facilities.

The most space-saving, though drastic method is to grade your clients according to size, then, using a well-sharpened saw, cut through the middle at the waist. Make sure that they are well frozen before starting to avoid clogging the blade. Separate the halves and hollow them out, using a broad chisel and a wooden mallet. Starting with the smallest, fit the next largest person over it and repeat with each size until you have fitted the largest. This way you will be able to fit an impressive number of bodies into the space normally occupied by one, much like those wooden Russian dolls. Do keep a note, however, of who is where in the stack in case anyone asks to see one of the clients. Without a handy record you may have no alternative but to disassemble your entire stock, with the attendant risk of mixing up the various top and bottom halves.

Once you have equipped yourself with a stock of freezers, there are other business opportunities open to you such as a 'spare parts' service to hospitals.

freezer room should have a small window sprayed with canned plastic snow sufficiently thick to obscure the view, while a few winking lights on a panel above the door look particularly impressive. The panel can easily be constructed from ½in plywood with ¼in quadrant beading to finish off the edges.

The most profitable area of cryogenics is certainly the storage of people who have died of some incurable disease. The idea is to store them until a cure has been found, at which point they can be thawed out and treated. A neat concept but one which is actually highly unlikely to work, though this is actually immaterial as there are lots of clients who are willing to take the chance.

One of the main problems you will encounter is the fact that very few

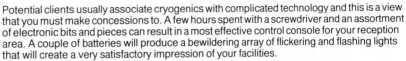

METHODS

A

Potential clients usually associate cryogenics with complicated technology and this is a view that you must make concessions to. A few hours spent with a screwdriver and an assortment of electronic bits and pieces can result in a most effective control console for your reception area. A couple of batteries will produce a bewildering array of flickering and flashing lights that will create a very satisfactory impression of your facilities.

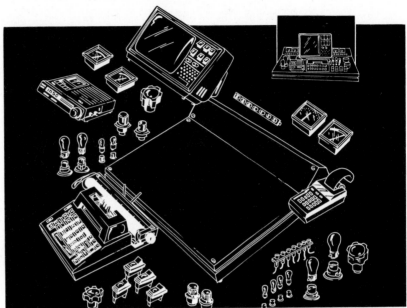

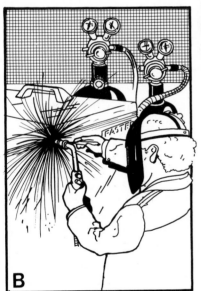

B

Storage of cadavers can be a problem should close friends or relatives decide to pay the corpse a visit. To get round this difficulty without the extravagant use of storage space or the ignominy of sorting through stacks of frozen clients, it is worth considering the following idea:

(a) Take two chest freezers and, using a hacksaw or metal cutters, remove the front from each without damaging the lids.

(b) Placing them opposite each other so that the two open fronts are butted up together, weld the two freezers into one large unit.

(c) After making sure that the lids open and close satisfactorily, firmly fix the new unit to

a steel or wooden drum using three or four inch coachbolts.

(d) The entire assembly can now be fixed to a stout, centrally mounted wall pivot. Fit an industrial rubber belt around the edge of the wood or steel drum with enough slack to allow you to pass it around a second, smaller drum fitted with a good-sized handle. Clients can be stacked head to toe in the most economic way and rotated to a vertical position for display purposes. Note that the electrical supply lead will have to be disconnected during rotation. You must remember to reconnect the supply once the freezer is positioned correctly to avoid the disconcerting sight of the loved one gradually wilting forward and getting soggy.

C

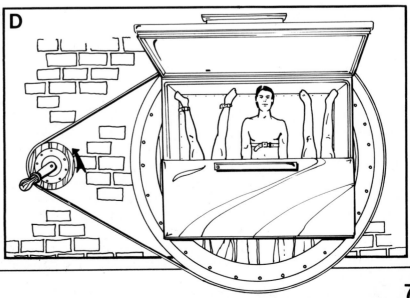

D

How to contact the Spirit World

YOU WILL NEED
A dark room,
One large table and
   set of chairs,
Incense.
A spirit trumpet,
Penetrating eyes,
Ectoplasm,
A private detective.

Before You Start

Cultivate an aquaintance with your local priest. Sometimes things can go wrong and a standby exorcist is good insurance. Learn a few Egyptian/Indian/German words and phrases.

One of the most important things to acquire when setting up as a medium or spiritualist is an expression of humble wisdom, to stress the impression that, despite your preference for a perfectly normal life, you embody, by divine accident, qualities which enable you to act as an intermediary between the worlds of the living and the dead. Allow your expression to suggest that it is actually a considerable inconvenience but one which you feel obliged to accept in view of the rarity of your 'gift'. When challenged as to the legitimacy of your activities, look sorrowful and murmur such phrases as 'Oh, would that it were but a shallow deception,' or 'How I envy you your role as a shoe salesman. It must be wonderful to live entirely in the everyday world.' A wan smile followed by the words 'I can see how difficult it must be for you to accept what you cannot understand' is also a useful one.

Your air of spiritual preoccupation should be reflected in the working environment which your clients will enter. Furnishings should be rather outdated in style, with lots of swathes of cloth and Art Nouveau decoration, while a thick layer of dust will reinforce the impression that your attentions are elsewhere most of the time. This will also help to make your clients feel that you are not in this for the money and have little care for worldly things.

When meeting a prospective customer, allow your attention to wander once or twice, staring intently into space. His conversation will falter, and after a pause you can give a quick shake of the head, apologize and ask him what he was saying. You can explain that you were distracted by a 'presence'. If you add that the strength of his aura disturbs you, you will almost certainly clinch the deal.

Contacting dead relatives represents the bulk of your business and,

though tedious, is good bread-and-butter stuff. Before your first appointment with a client, use your private detective to do as much preliminary research as possible to enable you to intersperse your improvizations with plenty of actual references. Do not use them all up too quickly!

The actual séance should be conducted in the gloom, seated at a draped table with a single soft light directly above. Spend the first few minutes of the session emitting low moans with occasional bouts of heavy breathing. Be careful not to overdo the latter in case the customer suddenly becomes convinced that you are in the throes of a coronary and panics. This is particularly important if you indicate contact with the other world by suddenly slumping apparently senseless in your chair. Telling the customer in advance that he should not be alarmed at what is to occur is not always sufficient.

A popular precedent to the actual contact, particularly if you are proposing to go for a manifestation, is the introduction of ectoplasm, the raw

Above
If you are really serious about learning the correct techniques, it is worth going to some of the many spiritualist seminars and competitions to observe how the experts do it. Many useful hints can be gleaned from events such as this ectoplasm-emitting contest.

Facing Page
Once you have mastered the basic skills you can begin to introduce those little innovations that will distinguish you from your competitors in the field. A fine example of a personal trademark is this luminous beard devised by Swami Archie Proctor of Dallas, Texas.

Overleaf
An easy-to-make setup of special effects for the novice medium. Although very effective with first-time clients or the particularly gullible, it will not appear convincing to those with wider experience. As your clients will, hopefully, make use of your services on future occasions you must regard this suggested layout as a temporary one only.

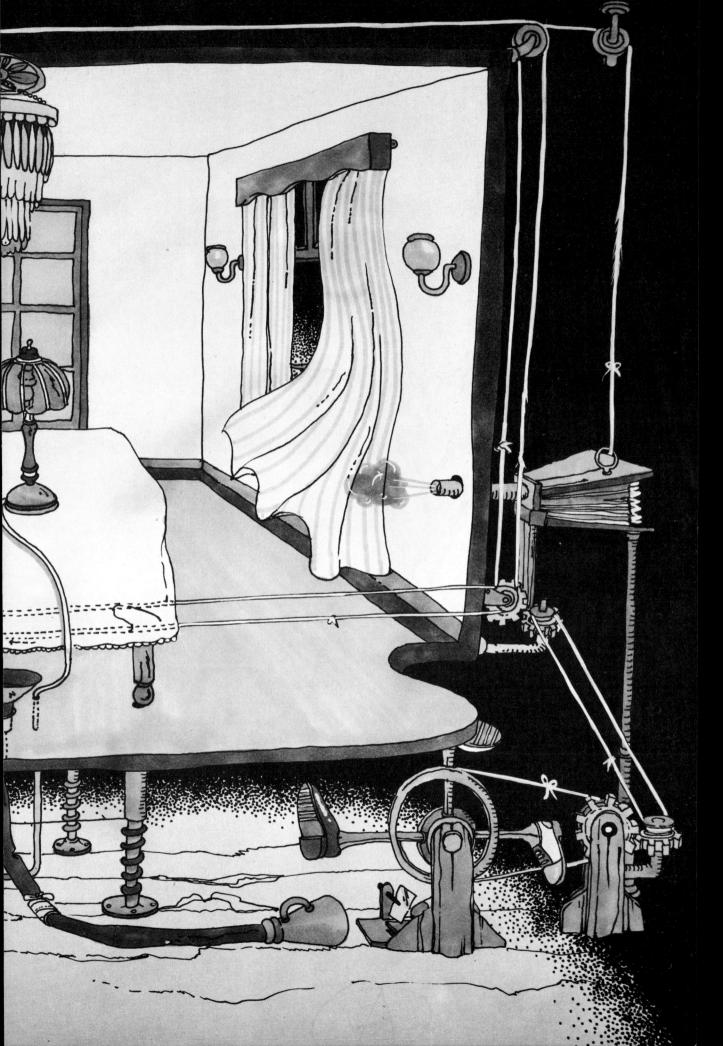

To confound disbelievers, this photograph shows the ghost of the Vicomtesse d'Autoroute ascending the staircase of the ancestral home at Vichy sur Perrier.

cellular matter drawn from the medium out of which the spirit adopts a material form. This can be fashioned from a variety of substances, but latex is one of the most versatile. Although some practitioners prefer making it appear from the nose or ears, this does require considerable skill and the novice is better advised to use the mouth.

Experience will teach you how much to produce and the best speed. Too slow a rate could lead to suffocation, a dramatic if uncomfortable way of concluding a séance; too fast and your client may decide that you have been abruptly and energetically taken ill, with the result that the mood will have been destroyed. This could be most inconvenient if he leaps to your aid and you are faced with the problem of disposing of the 'ectoplasm' at short notice. You could, in such circumstances, try shrieking and hurling the lump of material out of the nearest window, proclaiming that it is a malevolent spirit, but you will have to retrieve it before your client departs, as he might recognize it.

Assuming, however, that you have mastered the basic techniques, make sure that the ectoplasm is fixed to a fine black thread by which it can be whisked up through a small aperture in the ceiling as a preliminary to the next stage. The actual manifestation can be achieved through careful lighting of a suitably attired accomplice, a moving muslin shroud or, for wealthy mediums, a laser-light 3D projection or hologram.

Careful preparation can provide a selection of mysteriously moving objects such as chairs, tables, magic trumpets and the like, but do make certain that they are properly arranged as otherwise they may have the opposite effect to that which is intended. A client struck heavily by a falling trumpet will not be disposed to continue the session with the appropriate degree of equanimity.

When actually relaying messages from the spirit world (which do not, incidentally, have to make any sense at all) adopt as different a tone of voice as possible to make it clear that it is not you that is speaking. The exact nature of the voice is up to you, but avoid using such ploys as talking like Donald Duck as spirits do not really sound like that in the popular imagination. Practise talking without moving your lips for several hours a week before you conduct your first session. If you are not confident of your ability in this direction, it is best to slump forward

a

Inspiration from beyond the grave is always a good way to supplement your income and have some amusement. There is no harm in going for the better-known personalities such as Rembrandt (a) or Beethoven (b) as they are the easiest to research.
A few hours each week spent studying such examples of your chosen subject's work as this page from Beethoven's *Erotica* (c) manuscript will not go amiss. You will then be in a position to knock out some quite respectable works attributable to your subject and transmitted through you from the other side.

b

onto the table to obscure your lips, but leave enough room to prevent the voice being too muffled.

Once you have established a reputation as a medium, all sorts of other opportunities will present themselves. One of the most appealing is to declare yourself the mortal instrument of some famous and long dead artist, musician or writer. A familiarity with the works of your chosen guide is very useful, but any lack of personal proficiency apparent in the works relayed from beyond the grave can be passed off as the result of your natural limitations in transferring the supernatural stimuli to their physical form. Some basic ability is desirable, however. There is little point in electing to become the transcriber of Beethoven's latest works if you known absolutely nothing about music. Similarly, Rembrandt is unlikely

to feel compelled to alter his style to that of stick-figures.

If you are apprehensive about communicating with humans, why don't you specialize in doing so with animals? The contacting of deceased pets is also much easier to arrange effectively. Very, very few pets actually talked to their owners much, so you are free to improvize. Even in the case of garrulous parrots you can explain that, freed of their mortal bodies, they no longer need or desire to be restricted to the few phrases they could manage while alive. Their 'messages' can, therefore, take any form you please and will invariably delight and comfort their earthly owners.

If, in the course of building up your career, you actually succeed in contacting the spirit world, consult a qualified medium immediately.

c

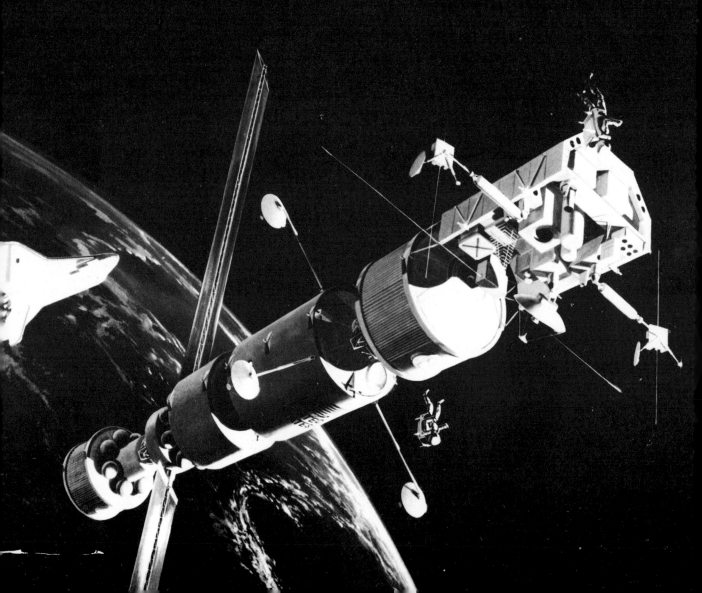

ORBITAL HARDWARE FROM THE HOME WORKSHOP

Before You Start

You will need to have a fairly well-stocked toolbox if you intend to construct much of the equipment yourself. A soldering iron is essential. When launching an orbital vehicle, stand well back as they get *very* hot. If you intend to enter orbit yourself, do take some provisions and a flask of something warming; you will be surprised just how cold space can be.

A childhood dream or a strong sense of adventure is often all it takes to spur the ordinary individual into making his personal contribution to Man's exploration of space. Most people, however, are put off by what they imagine to be the staggering cost of placing objects in orbit. Little do they realize how cheaply, in fact, it can be done. More important still, the advantages, or what have become generally known as the 'spin-offs' of acquiring orbital capacity can, if imaginatively employed, recoup your initial outlay in a remarkably short time. From then on the financial rewards can be impressive.

Man is becoming increasingly dependent on the services offered by orbital facilities: weather forecasting, communications, geophysical research, navigational aids and so on. The field of espionage alone offers all sorts of opportunities for the enterprising do-it-yourselfer. Scientific establishments all over the world are only too willing to pay for the chance to see what kind of webs spiders make in space and other important experiments, and by taking bookings in advance you can get your own space program 'off the ground' without having to dip into your own savings.

The first thing you need is obviously a rocket powerful enough to place a useful payload in earth orbit. If you have the means, it is quite possible to acquire a reliable, rust-free used Saturn V or similar, but for most people this is not practicable. Do not despair, however, for rockets are essentially surprisingly simple things, and with a bit of ingenuity and a lot of hard work you can build a perfectly serviceable example yourself.

It will have to be pretty large as you will need to be able to generate about half to three-quarters of a million pounds of thrust in order to reach escape velocity (about 18,000 mph). Unless your rocket reaches this speed it will almost certainly fall back to earth before attaining an orbit, an event which would be not only disappointing but also dangerous, as rockets are extremely heavy. Most of the bulk will, of course, consist of fuel tanks, for to produce the necessary amount of thrust your rocket will consume about 15 tons of propellant every second.

Probably the best fuel to go for is a kerosene and oxygen mixture, as any surplus of the former can be used in your domestic oil heaters or for cleaning paint brushes. Surplus oxygen can be used by anyone in the family wanting to do some extra breathing, or can be put aside for other projects (see bathysphere).

You will need to build at least two engines to power all the stages of the launch vehicle, but you might as well make more while you're at it. They should have two fuel inlets, one for the kerosene and one for the oxygen, as the two are not

Above
If looking for a ready-made launch vehicle it is worth considering the rugged and reliable Saturn V. Although produced in quite large numbers making spares less of a problem, they have been in service some time so make sure that you do not land yourself with an old example that has been quietly rusting away on a Cape Kennedy backlot.

Facing Page
Sam and Joey Jackson of Idaho enjoy a game of hide-and-seek in the back yard of their family's weekend home near Mars.

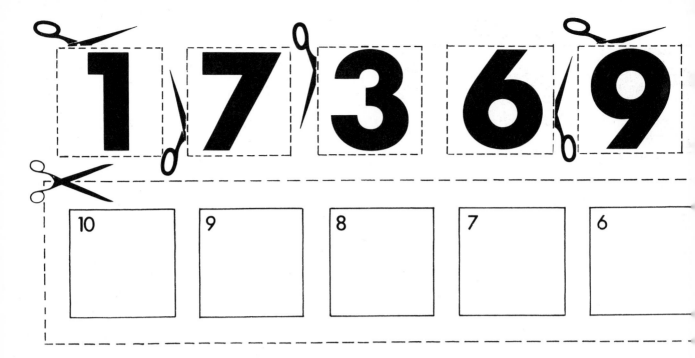

An accurate countdown is a vital part of any launch. Cut out each of the numbers as indicated and stick them in correct order in the boxes provided. Cut out the whole strip to make yourself a precise and efficient 'countdown console'.

mixed until the combustion stage. A pump for each should be fitted to pressurize the igniters where the fuel will burn. At one end of the combustion chamber, you should leave a narrow aperture for the expanding gases to escape through the expansion nozzle. Do not overlook this detail unless your are planning to destroy the district.

The outer surface of the hull which will carry the engines should be made as smooth as possible to reduce air resistance, and you will need to invest in some pressure-sensitive relays to detach each stage as it is exhausted. Use a reliable electronic calculator to work out the amount of fuel you will need to attain your intended orbit and you will avoid any wastage.

Do plan ahead when launch day is drawing near, as it will be too late to have second thoughts regarding the nature of your payload once the countdown has been completed and you have ignition. A useful tip is to ignore the popular practice of counting down from ten, and start at a much higher number. You will then have some leeway in which to reconsider if you wish. An orbital shot is always fairly expensive and a few extra moments of contemplation can avoid a costly error.

If you plan to make a number of launches to place objects in space, it is really worth considering the slightly greater outlay of constructing a reusable space shuttle. Though you will have to control your desire to get something up as soon as possible, it will save you a lot of time and trouble in the long run. A shuttle of this kind will pose a few additional problems such as the provision of a suitable landing point for its return, but provided that they can be overcome you will be able to make very substantial savings in your operating costs.

Having your own shuttle not only reduces the cost of each launch but also makes access to your orbital hardware much easier. Flying lessons will have to be included in your budget, of course, but if you put a little extra aside each week, you will be surprised how quickly they can be paid for. If you have other friends who are also planning to launch their own satellites, etc., it is worth getting together to share the extra cost in return for the shuttle's services.

One particularly exciting possibility offered by a shuttle is the construction of an orbital space station. Materials and workers can be ferried into orbit by the craft and the station can be built very easily on site, as it were. Because you won't have to allow for gravity, the construction can employ very light materials such as cooking foil and sheets of corrugated iron, most of which can be carried up in a single journey. Because there is no up or down out there, you can make the

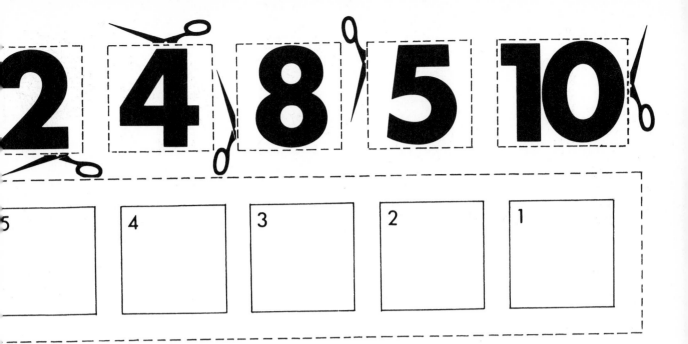

2 4 8 5 10

5 4 3 2 1

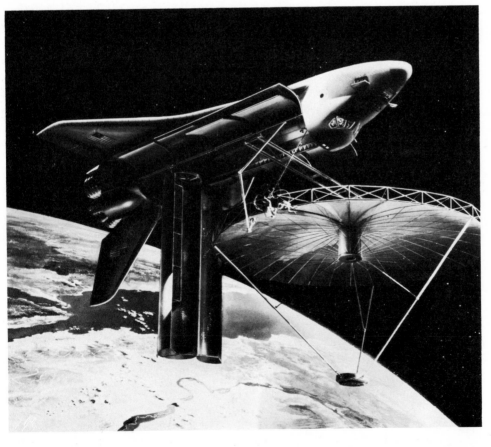

Left
Building a replica Space Shuttle is an excellent long-term investment if you intend to make a number of trips into orbit, and will justify the high initial cost. It has the advantage of offering ample accommodation and storage space for those extra items of luggage that can make all the difference to an orbital vacation.

design a simple cylinder closed at each end, with the internal facilities placed anywhere round the interior. This will make the maximum use of the available space. Do not omit to place plenty of handholds at strategic points to stop occupants flying around inside.

When constructing the space station, take care to wear a spacesuit at all times. These should be tough but flexible; a puncture could be fatal, but it is important to be able to move your arms and legs. Wear plenty of warm garments underneath as space is very, very cold indeed and as there is no air there, you

will need to carry some with you. If using a water circulating system to provide warmth, make sure that the heater is fitted with a thermostat to avoid your suit filling up with steam or bursting. Both are undesirable.

Apart from allowing you to carry out a host of interesting scientific investigations like taking photographs of clouds, an orbital station can double as a holiday home for the ultimate in getaway vacations. Do remember, however, when considering going outside, that it is important to be able to get in again. Use either a tether line fixed securely to the station, or carry a small propulsion unit; an ordinary aerosol will do, and make sure that any accompanying pet is kept on a leash at all times. Incidentally, space's inherent quality of easily precipitated movement must be borne in mind at all times. Take care, for example, when using the personal waste facilities to remember the principle of equal and opposite reactions, and make sure you have a firm grip on a secure fixture to avoid startling your colleagues with a dramatic and inadvertent fly-past.

Space is an alien and unforgiving environment, but if reasonable care is taken at all times, it can offer a great deal of pleasure and the opportunity to generate very useful profits. Always treat it with respect and never go into orbit without telling others of your family where you are going in case your do run into difficulties. Observing all the basic safety rules will ensure that every orbital trip is a happy one.

Facing Page
Sheathing your craft in heat absorbent tiles not only protects the occupants during re-entry but also allows you to personalize your own spacecraft with a wide range of decorative finishes. Do remember, however, to carry a few spare tiles and some adhesive on board to replace any lost during the launch. Press the tiles firmly in place before grouting.

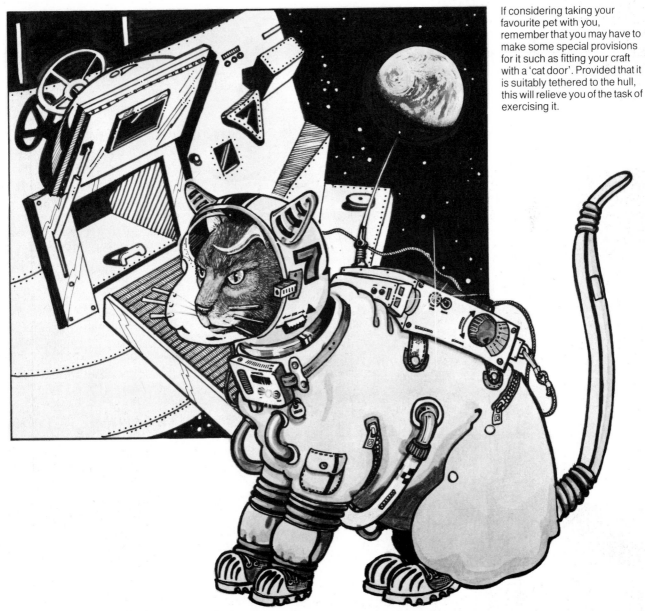

If considering taking your favourite pet with you, remember that you may have to make some special provisions for it such as fitting your craft with a 'cat door'. Provided that it is suitably tethered to the hull, this will relieve you of the task of exercising it.

SAVE CASH WITH HYDRO=ELECTRICS

You will need

A reliable water source
Some large magnets
Plenty of copper wire
A transformer
A large dam
A wheelbarrow

Before You Start

Consider carefully the proximity of your water source to the place where you want the generated power. Power cable is expensive and the further apart the two places, the longer it will take to recoup your initial outlay. Never forget that electricity is highly dangerous, so do not just poke around inside complicated hydro-electrics at random and never hold wires if you're wet.

Getting a spark

As much electricity as you can use for free! Too good to be true, you may think, but it is a dream than can become reality. Electricity is pretty mysterious stuff and is usually completely invisible, which can also make it dangerous when there is a lot of it on the loose. As a result a lot of folk do not like to mess around with it, and flicking a switch is as close to it as they want to get. But quite apart from the enormous saving in your household budget that can be achieved, generating your own electricity can be fun.

The first thing to establish is your prime water source, and this may involve a bit of searching around. It is worth investing in a good map because these often show where some water is. First find out where you are by seeing if there are names on the map that you recognize and marking the spot with a pencil. Do not use ink in case you are wrong and have to start again. Once you have established your position, you can look for water by finding all the blue marks on the map, then follow the roads that will take you to the area. Once you feel that you are quite close, keep a sharp look-out for the actual water, but be warned, it will quite often appear completely different from the blue shown on your map.

Once the water has been discovered you must look for movement in it. Waves do not really count but a current is very useful. Take note of that last word, it will crop up rather a lot when you begin constructing the electrical equipment. Electricity is very like water in some ways and often behaves in a similar fashion. It can be channelled through wires as water can

a

b

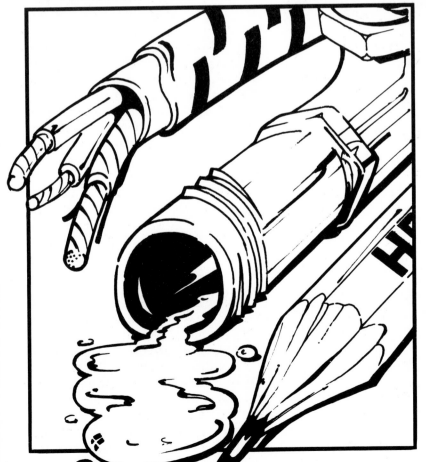

Above

Identifying types of water is especially important in hydro-electrics, as some kinds of water are less efficient than others.

(a) This is a good example of 'still water' which is generally unsuitable for the production of electricity.

(b) Running water can be identified by its corrugated surface. This surface texture can also provide a clue as to the size of the water area as larger expanses will often exhibit a regular surface pattern called 'waves'.

Left

Although there are many similarities between water and electricity there are some vital differences. Both can be passed from one point to another through tubular conduits but the types of carrier are NOT interchangeable! A wire (top) carries electricity and is not hollow enough to pass much water through. A pipe (middle), on the other hand, has a hole through the middle to carry water but electricity will not flow along it. Also shown here is a pencil (bottom) which passes neither electricity nor water despite the physical similarities.

Having selected your site, constructed a dam and installed your hydro-electric turbine you will need to lay enough cable to carry the power to your house. Your rate of production will probably exceed your domestic consumption much of the time, so it is worth constructing a large storage tank to keep all your surplus electricity. This can then be retained for periods of especially heavy consumption or even for sale.

flow through pipes, but do not confuse the two types of carrier. An easy guide is to remember that wires do not have a hole through the middle and are often thinner. Pipes and wires are not interchangeable so do not try to pour water down the latter; it is pointless.

If your most convenient water supply lacks the current to drive the generator turbine, do not despair, for it is possible to construct a simple device to block up the stream or river and thus increase the amount of controllable pressure. This is called a dam, and can be rather tricky to make. Just shovelling in a lot of soil rarely works, as it is easily washed away. Throw in plenty of large rocks instead, and pour concrete over the top, making the upper edge higher than the intended water level. Water is slippery stuff and failure to build the dam high enough will allow the water to slide over the top. Leave a hole at the bottom of the dam through which the water will squirt at high speed to provide the energy needed to spin the turbine.

Take a long, stout shaft and mount it very firmly at the ends. Using a strong grade of sheet steel, cut out several fair-sized squares and fix them firmly to the end of the shaft nearest the water. When the water is released the shaft will spin at high speed.

Place two very large magnets at the opposite end of the shaft to the water. These will generate a magnetic field in which the coil will spin to produce the electricity. You should make your generator as big as you can as you should really aim to generate around 100,000 Kilowatts of power, which would satisfy your own domestic needs with enough to spare to supply others. Try to find your customers from a single area so as to avoid having to lay expensive power lines all over the countryside. A lot of people consider them unsightly. A useful tip which can lead to a little extra income is to set baskets directly beneath the overhead lines to catch any ready-fried birds.

Before starting any electrical engineering work it is worth familiarizing yourself with some of the correct terminology. We have already mentioned the word current, but there are others equally important. One is Watt, a word which underlines the mysterious nature of electricity and is a measure of power. Another is Volt, which according to the dictionary means 'the gait of a horse going sideways round a centre' which is still more mysterious. Other key words are plug, meaning putting wires in holes; terminal, meaning you are about to make an important mistake; cable, meaning to send a telegram for help when you have; and switch, meaning to change your mind about the whole thing.

Armed with these words, two different sizes of screwdriver and a pair of rubber boots you are ready to bring light and warmth into the homes of thousands.

Once the dam has been completed you can begin constructing the actual generating equipment. This will consist of two main parts; the turbine which is basically a large propeller spinning in the water flow, and the main generator itself. The latter should be built around the propeller shaft as it will otherwise not work at all.

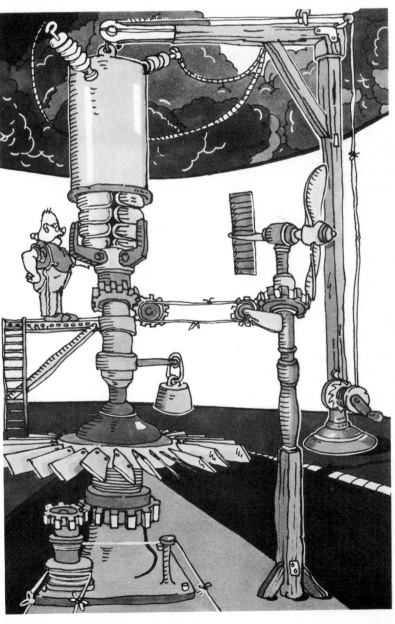

15

CONVERT YOUR HOME TO A ROMANTIC RUIN

You will need.

A house
A good supply of water
A shovel
100,000 termites
6 breeding pairs of bats
Several large tents
Somewhere to live

Before You Start

Try and get a good idea of what you intend the final appearance to be rather than improvize as you proceed. Once structural modifications have been made to the fabric of the building it is difficult and expensive to rectify. If in doubt, consult an architect.

Here is a superb example of a hand-crafted ruin illustrating good use of ivy, window frames stripped of protective paintwork and strategically removed roof cladding. If these preparatory stages are well executed, time and the elements very quickly take their toll to produce a home you can be proud of.

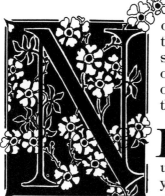o-one likes his home to be just like every other one in the locality. Thus, from the moment people take possession of a new house, they tend to impose their own tastes on it and make improvements that will increase the value of the property. The cost of such ventures is very high and the work itself is often disrupting to the daily routine.

But there is a far easier way to endow your home with a unique and dramatic character, without having to invest your hard-earned savings in expensive materials and specialist craftsmen. Nor will you have to acquire a host of practical skills. With the minimum outlay and a few hours you can convert your house to a romantic and highly individual ruin that will attract a great deal of envious attention.

People travel miles to view ruins and the majestic nobility that emanates from their time-worn, ivy-clad fabric, be they ancient cathedrals or derelict cottages. This is the quality that you should seek to capture in your own dwelling. The method of carrying out the work will depend on your available time; if the latter is in short supply you can let nature and the elements do much of the work.

All you have to do is to provide a starting point for these forces to do their work. Start by removing about 20 per cent of the slates or tiles on the roof, making certain that any waterproof covering beneath is pierced or cut.

The most demanding part of the work will be digging out beneath the exterior walls to undermine the foundations. This must be done carefully to ensure that enough soil has been removed to encourage settlement of the structure. A useful tip here is to pump in plenty of water once you have removed as much soil as you can. Pretty soon you should be able to spot some impressive settlement cracks running vertically from the foundations to the roof line.

Now is the time to plant your ivy. Pack plenty of rich compost into the widening cracks and plant your cuttings, using the heel of your hand to bed them in firmly. Once these have taken they will begin to force their way into the cracks and loosen the brick or stonework in a most authentic fashion.

Next, use a blowtorch to remove as much as possible of all exterior paintwork to let the weather do its work. If you have the time, use a masonry chisel to chip away the cement around the window frames, and work the frames loose, as this will help to accelerate the process of rot.

If you anticipate some really frosty weather, run a hose up to the loft and, wedging the nozzle firmly, allow it to pour a continuous stream of water down the exterior walls. This will find its way into all the various cracks and crevices, where it will freeze. Any external rendering will soon start to fall away in patches, creating a striking effect that is almost impossible to duplicate by simply chipping it away. If you also pierce a few holes in the part of the hose that lies inside the house, and leave it there permanently, you will be amazed at how quickly the floor joists and plasterwork begin to decay.

Before long the resulting damp will create some really stunning effects. The huge variety of fungi that will proliferate will offer a breathtaking display of nature at work, and will provide you with a most effective conversation piece when you have guests. You will not have to do anything very much to damage your interior decor as it will be no more than a few days before the wallpapers begin to rot away and the ceilings begin to sag and fall, exposing the attractive pattern of laths beneath.

This method does take some time before nature has fully played its part, and if you have a little extra money to spend you can do a great deal to accelerate the process. The effects of subsidence, for example, can be duplicated within a few hours by digging out the foundations as described earlier, but instead of allowing settlement to occur spontaneously, rent two or three heavy-duty hydraulic jacks from a tool rental company and place them at strategic points beneath the building. Raise and lower them as quickly as possible a number of times and you will see the structural fabric of the building begin to disintegrate almost immediately. Do not, however, overdo this stage as it will be difficult removing the jacks in the event of the house collapsing completely.

Once you have achieved the desired effect you can erect your large tents in those rooms which you use frequently, to provide a measure of protection from dripping water and falling plasterwork. Now your joy should be complete.

METHODOLOGY

Left

Inadequate foundations are essential to the creation of a romantic ruin. Unfortunately most houses constructed in the last few decades usually have quite solid foundations so you will need to dig these out. Placing a very strong jack beneath the outer walls and alternately lifting and dropping the structure will help considerably and can produce some spectacular effects.

Right

A thick covering of ivy is a prerequisite for any good quality ruin and much can be done to enhance and speed up the ravages of time.
(a) First use a broad-bladed cold chisel to cut a deep, narrow trench in the outer brickwork.

(b) Using steel or hardwood wedges driven into the crack, create a good sized fissue and clean out most of the resulting brick fragments.

(c) Pack the crevice with good loamy soil or potting compost and embed a handful of ivy seeds or small plants.

(d) Plant nutrients will encourage healthy growth and, once well established, the ivy will carry on the work of undermining the structural fabric of your home as well as putting forth a rich cluster of attractive, glossy foliage.

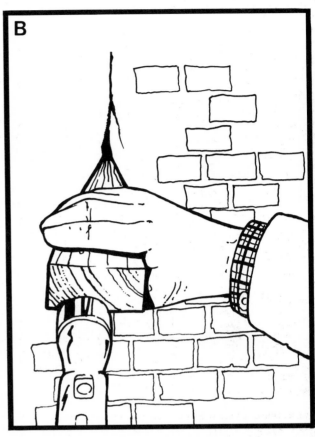

16 NOUVELLE CUISINE TERMINALE

You will need

A large oven
Tables & chairs
Smart menus
A wheelbarrow

Before You Start

Spend some moments in meditative repose.

The world is full of famous chefs and some of them can cook, so be prepared for stiff competition.

The problem is to find a way of becoming famous in the shortest possible time and here, as with many things, it is a case of finding a speciality with which to rock the culinary establishment. Some chefs have risen to prominence by creating new styles of food preparation: traditional, country-style, ethnic, and more recently from France, *Cuisine Minceur* (cooking with mince).

At first glance there seems little opportunity left for the aspiring famous chef to exploit a new way of preparing dishes, but this is not so. One area which has scarcely been touched is cooking for the thousands of people whose passion for elegant cookery is cruelly frustrated by a serious weight problem. Every attempt to exploit this enormous market has failed to provide the logical answer as even the most effectively calorie-controlled foods are fattening if you eat huge amounts of them. Open the first *Cuisine Torture* restaurant and you're really in business, for no client will put on an ounce after eating such gourmet delicacies as *Pneu Farci aux Gommes*.

Pneu Farci aux Gommes

To prepare this succulent dish, you will need the following: One tyre (with tube), flour, light machine oil, and for the stuffing: 9 ounces of chopped erasers, 3 ounces of elastic bands, 2 tablespoons of milk, 1½ ounces of margarine, salt and pepper.

Cut the tyre into as many individual portions as needed and remove the inner tube from each. Do not throw this away. Dip each portion in flour and brown lightly in the machine oil. Season with salt and pepper. Next finely chop the extracted inner tube and mix in well with the stuffing ingredients making sure that the elastic bands are cut into fairly small pieces. When thoroughly mixed, spread the stuffing thickly inside the portions of tyre and close them with metal skewers. Place in a baking dish, baste with more machine oil at intervals and cook for 30-35 minutes at 350°F. Serve individually on a bed of polystyrene granules.

To contrast with the tangy taste and perfume of this uniquely tormenting dish, an excellent starter would be acrylic resin and beef soup (*Potage de boeuf et raisins*). Tantilizingly good, it is surprisingly easy to make, the only disadvantage being that you will have to make it up as individual portions. It does keep indefinitely so make a good batch at one time. Mix the required quantity of acrylic resin with the correct quantity of hardener as stated on the container, and pour into the dishes. Drop in precooked cubes of prime beef, which will sink to the bottom. Place all the dishes to one side for not less than one hour to make sure that the resin has completely hardened. Any less than this and your customers might succeed in extracting the beef.

As an alternative, you could turn your attentions to the hapless thousands of people who have decided that existing is not worthwhile. *Cuisine Terminale* offers almost unlimited opportunities for you to exploit your culinary genius undisturbed by competition. *Omelette aux Rasoirs*, *Escalopes de Veau aux Broquettes* (veal escalopes stuffed with tacks), and *Homard Pourri Sauce Poudrée* (putrescent lobster in a powdered glass sauce) offer new gastronomic experiences as well as an easy way out for your patrons.

It is important to bear in mind when you are planning the daily menus that suicide is a very private exercise and your selections should offer a quiet, unobtrusive exit. It is quite outside the spirit of your specialized field to produce items which will spatter the other customers with blood, make loud and intrusive noises, or prematurely terminate other clients who have not yet dined, or worse still, not yet paid. Incidentally, bills should always be settled in advance as going

through the pockets of your late customers at the end of their meal is unseemly for an artiste of your stature.

For private parties, however, you can seize the opportunity to prepare special dishes of a more indiscriminate nature, bearing in mind only that you may want to use the restaurant again. On these occasions you can go for some very dramatic effects such

as are produced by dishes like *Landmine en Croûte* and a literal variation of *Bombe Surprise*. If anticipating group bookings of this kind it is wise to plan your décor accordingly; stainless steel tiles are both durable and can easily be hosed down at the end of the evening.

Another more specialized market which is inadequately catered for is that represented by

Entrée
Mud and Putty Vol-au-Vent

When baking your pastry shell, blend in an equal amount of linseed-oil putty before rolling out, and bake for less than a minute on a low heat. Mix the mud with a whole diced lemon and the white of an egg, place in a pan and bring to the boil. Pour into the pastry cases and serve immediately.

Main Course
Vulture Chasseur

Take one well hung elderly vulture. Heat ½lb of fly-specked butter and two tablespoons of cod liver oil in a large pan, add the vulture and brown lightly on all sides. Pour on a cup of petroleum spirit and flambée until the flames have subsided then add ¼ pint of maple syrup and beef stock, season with four tablespoons salt, rosemary and 12 cloves of garlic. Cook over a moderate heat for seven minutes before stirring in two tablespoons of anchovy paste and reducing the heat. Simmer for a further five minutes then serve with button mushrooms tossed in a sour cream and custard sauce.

those people just outside the previous category, who do not wish to deliberately take their own lives but who enjoy undergoing a really dreadful experience. There are no comparable establishments, so you will draw your customers from far afield. Your fame will allow you to select the evening's fare without alternative and an ideal menu is described below.

The willingness to innovate and a callous disregard for your fellow man are all that is required to make your name a household word for creative cookery. Throughout the rarified world of *Haute Cuisine* your reputation will be known, and publishers will flock from every corner of the world in their anxiety to secure the dispensation of your wisdom. You will naturally excite a certain

amount of professional jealousy but do not let criticism deflect you from your path. Every master chef who has contributed his creativity to the sum of culinary knowledge has been exposed to the ridicule of his less original colleagues. Such is the price of genius.

Dessert – Petites Bombes à la Gelée

Make as many solid balls of tart pastry as there are guests and cut a hollow centre in each. Pour in garlic butter and roll round to coat the interior. Once this has congealed pour in a mixture of peanut butter and Rocquefort cheese until full, then close with a pastry lid. Place all the *Bombes* in a large dish and fill with gelatine, placing the dish in the refrigerator until the gelatine has set. Immediately prior to serving, grate bitter chocolate over the dish, top off with Parmesan cheese and warm under the grill.

Presentation is everything in **Cuisine Horrible.**

17

YOU WILL NEED

A DOUBLE BREASTED SUIT
WITH PADDED SHOULDERS

A HAT

SPATS (optional)

A LARGE COLLEAGUE

A HUNDREDWEIGHT OF CEMENT

BEFORE YOU START

Learn to speak moving only one side
of the mouth. Practise first by
immobilizing one side with adhesive
tape or a stapler. Learn to walk
without moving the top half of your
body. Imagine that you are on castors.

Successful racketeering depends very much
on establishing a reputation and acquiring
a dauntingly sinister aura.

COATS? THEN BECOME A....

Spend some time each day in front of a
mirror learning the basic range of facial
expressions that you will need to employ.
The most important thing to cultivate is a
total lack of expression with every muscle
rigidly immobile, and the eyes flat and
expressionless. This one provides a basis for
most of the others in the professional repertoire.
Anger is denoted only by clenching the jaw muscles
and narrowing the eyes. Do not overdo the
latter or people will think you have accidentally
gone to sleep.

A second useful variation is to emit a staccato
series of grunts while maintaining the
standard expression. This is the Mirthless or
Hollow Laugh, and is very useful when you
cannot think of an answer to a question. Try
to make an exit while doing it, as it is
difficult to maintain indefinitely. Do not forget
to remove your cigar or cigarette from your
mouth first, or you will find yourself in a
snowstorm of ash. Try to avoid having to remove
your hands from your coat pockets except when
letting one of them hover close to your inside
pocket in a meaningful way, but

continued overleaf

be cautious about performing this gesture in the company of other racketeers as they sometimes do actually carry firearms rather than rolled-up handkerchiefs.

A large colleague is vital equipment, but do try to get hold of the real thing. Stacked heels, standing on tiptoe or stilts are really only suitable on a temporary basis unless everyone else in the group is doing the same. The ideal companion should never have to speak unless your own voice is unusually high pitched. In any case, all conversations should be carried on in a soft monotone whatever the nature of the discussion.

Once you are confident about your outward manner and appearance you are ready to start racketeering, and the next thing to do is to decide on the nature of your operation. Get established in one area before seeking to

Racketeering is all about fear; invoking it in others while appearing entirely free from it yourself. It is therefore essential to have mastered the appropriate facial expression, and you must devote as much time as is necessary to achieve a good result. It will, after all, be the only expression you will ever need so it is worth getting it right.

Go for heavy lidded eyes, grimly set jaw and imperiously arched eyebrows. A slight curl to the upper lip is a useful touch it you can manage it but do not use it in public unless you are certain that you have mastered it. There is nothing less impressive than a poorly managed lip that goes badly out of control giving the impression of abrupt and total physical and emotional collapse.

muscle in on others. An easy way to start is to gain access to a plot of land on which you can place at least a score of delapidated motor cars, each polished as well as possible and with price stickers plastered over the windshields. They do not need to be capable of running as they are not really for sale. This is your 'front'. Set up a hut in a suitable place on the site and purchase some secondhand spraying equipment, screwdrivers and wrenches to enable you to carry on the real business of changing the paintwork and plates of stolen vehicles, preparing getaway cars and so on. Do remember that this is highly illegal, however, and should not be undertaken unless you want to be a criminal as well as a racketeer.

Once you have a 'front' there are plenty of activities in which to involve yourself, and one is bootlegging. In the old Prohibition days it was necessary to manufacture your own alcoholic concoctions, but things are much easier today and the acquisition of stock less tedious. All you need to do is purchase a sizeable quantity of a beverage such as whisky and place batches of bottles in a bath filled with warm water. Test the temperature by rolling up your sleeve and dipping the point of the elbow in the water.

After immersing the bottles for at least half an hour you should find that the proprietary labels are quite easy to remove. You can then write HOOCH or MACHINE OIL on plain adhesive labels and stick one on each bottle. While your colleague is busy with this job, you will have to do plenty of sidling and stepping out of shadows to find customers, not forgetting that all-important side-of-mouth technique. Make sure that you pitch your prices

A good 'front' to your illegitimate activities is most important. One of the most widely favoured fronts is the used car business and you should keep a lookout for something like the one shown here. Remember that you will not actually be conducting any business on these premises.

very low to wipe out the competition and to secure all the available customers in what will be known as your 'territory.' Fun though modern bootlegging is, do resist the temptation to do it too often or you will go broke through selling the whisky for much less that you paid for it.

The Protection Racket, on the other hand, can be very profitable indeed as there are plenty of people who will be happy to pay money to be protected. Baby-sitting, for example, can be extremely lucrative.

Gambling is also a worthwhile operation but it is better to run the various schemes yourself. Try to enlist the participation of others as you and your colleague will soon get bored with winning at your own rigged games. Always be ready to move out quickly as there will usually be some smart guy who will eventually spot that you are getting more than your fair share of 'Bank Error in Your Favour' cards in each Monopoly game.

Fixing horse races is a traditional stamping ground for racketeers and there are a host of opportunities for a quick profit. Put a little pressure on your local abattoir and take possession of a likely-looking carcass or complete hide. With a little preliminary work (see Taxidermy) you can fit the beast over a high-powered motorcycle and enter it as an outsider (a rank one unless you have prepared it adequately). Place your bets at the best odds and once the race is underway try to keep amongst the pack until the last furlong when you can pull ahead to be first over the line. Do not get too excited during the race as the larger motorcycles are capable of pretty astonishing speeds and crossing the line at 130 mph might attract unwelcome attention. Select the races with care and only go for flat races as using this technique for steeplechase events poses some considerable difficulties at the fences.

As you become more and more successful in the racketeering business you will find that many of your competitors will resent your progress and may attempt to 'rub you out.' This is the time for special caution; always look both ways before crossing the street and never, never run out after a ball from between parked cars. Make up a dummy from an old pair of pyjamas and straw, using indelible colours for the face to avoid leaving difficult marks on your sheets, and place it in your bed. You can then make up a snug little nest underneath with a small cardboard box to store some provisions to make it a real adventure.

There is always the possibility that you might wish to remove some of the opposition yourself. This can not only allow you to take over their territory to enlarge your operation, but can also be great fun. If you own a car, there is plenty of scope for some exciting chases, rammings, overturnings, squealing of tyres and shooting out of the windows. Restaurants and garages are the places in which to gun them down although the origins of this tradition are a little uncertain.

Probably the most acceptable method of disposing of your rivals is the use of the concrete overcoat which, although fairly straightforward, does require some preparation. Make sure that you have custody of your victim before making the 'overcoat' as it is extremely difficult to get him into it once it has set. Make up the correct mixture from three parts of coarse sand to one part of cement, mixing thoroughly before adding water a little at a time. Blend well until the mixture has a soft, buttery consistency.

Make up a simple case or former, placing the victim inside before adding the concrete. It is very difficult to avoid the use of such a mould as wet concrete is fairly fluid and if simply poured over the victim, will be inclined to slide off into a doughy lump on the floor. Once the concrete has set hard, strip off the wooden casing to reveal the neat, smooth concrete shape, which is much more pleasing to the eye. You will need suitable transportation to move the fairly weighty result to the nearest convenient river or lake where it can be disposed of.

Finally, if you persevere and work industriously at your trade, there is every chance that you will soon be mayor and get rid of all your rivals in one clean sweep. Once you have succeeded in this the world is your oyster and you are poised to enter politics.

As a racketeer, there will certainly be occasions when you will need to dispose of a competitor or 'grass', and you should have mastered the basic techniques of disposing of both the competitor and the evidence. The 'concrete overcoat' is one of the most effective methods. (a) First mix up a good batch of concrete, carefully blending three parts of sand to one of cement. (b) Construct a box slightly larger than the body to be disposed of, using plywood or blockboard at least ½″ thick. Fitting inexpensive drawer handles will make transportation easier later on. (c) Place the victim inside and pour in the mixture of concrete, making sure that it is evenly spread to avoid air pockets. (d) Once the concrete has hardened off completely, you can proceed with the actual disposal of the assembly by whatever means is most expedient.

18

Nobel Prize here I come
Inventing a miracle drug

You will need

A Swiss
bank account

You will also need

1/ A Swiss address
(preferably on snowy
mountain slopes)
3/ A pill making machine
and white powder
white coat and
surgical mask
A gross of white
mice
5/ White hair and an
earnest expression.

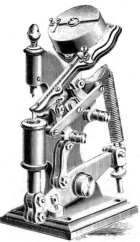

above
You will need a pill-making machine. A pre-owned example will do for your early efforts.

Left
Hair restorers sell well, but exaggerated claims are hard to live up to.

Far Left
A Swiss bank of the kind that you will need to contact in order to make provision for your staggering profits.

As can be seen from this collection of past Nobel Prize winners a certain style of presentation and facial expression is important. This is not to be confused with the style required for certain other professions (q.v. Be a Racketeer).

Facing Page
This is the sort of thing that happens if you are successful in introducing your miracle drug.

106

Before You Start

Medical research of international importance is a very clinical process and the more white things you have the more successful you will appear to be. Paradoxically, however, your skin should be deeply tanned (not necessary if you are black-skinned) to denote your excellent health and, by association, the excellence of your products.

It seems to be a fact that one of the most instantly profitable professions is also one of the easiest to establish. Miracle cures have long been an everyday part of medical life and people seem to bear no resentment towards them when they fail to live up to expectations; they are too busy being excited about the next miracle cure. Innovatory medicine is very similar to the pop music industry, though considerably easier to get into, and the hit parade of both businesses is constantly changing. This places extreme pressure on the existing research establishments to meet the demand.

Presentation is all-important, so do not skimp on the requirements listed above. Trying to save money by using domestic mice will only limit your success in the end. First you will need to identify a medical problem common to the majority of people. The common

cold, acne or travel sickness are ideal subjects, but do not opt for any cure purporting to treat any serious complaints as there is then a very real risk of disadvantageous repercussions.

The key to any major project will be the discovery of a miracle ingredient which should incorporate a number of popular characteristics. It would ideally be hailed as a spin-off from international space technology, made possible through the micro-chip, be derived from natural vegetable ingredients and, in view of the common faith that nothing really worthwhile is ever cheap, it should be incredibly expensive.

Medical testing will naturally be of paramount importance, for, without successful results, you will not gain the vital support of the international medical fraternity. You can perform and publish the results of these examinations yourself before passing the product on for official governmental testing while you get on with the business of producing, distributing and promoting your miracle drug.

By the time that the official results are through you will have made a fortune and will be developing the next contender for miracle drug of the month. Your own tests must, of course, be encouraging. If you intend to offer a medication that, overnight, makes acne a teenage misery of the past, for example, carry out the most searching and stringent test to make sure that

WORLD MAP SHOWING TAX HAVENS, SUBWAY ROUTES, NOT MUCH ELSE

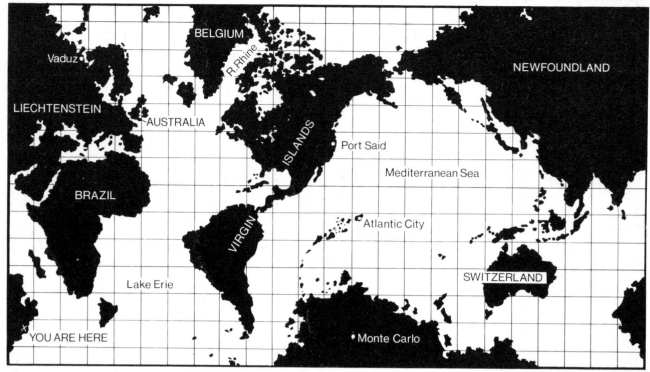

Above
An essential part of the miracle drug business is the occasional disappearance from the civilized world. You will need to have established a secret hideaway in some little known quarter. To assist you in locating a suitable refuge we have included this map of the world which includes some tax havens.

Right
Practice your handwriting, it is probably far too good right now.

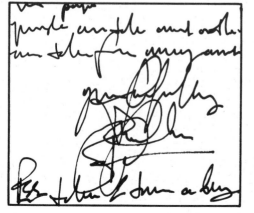

sheets and pillow cases will not only remain unmarked but will spin even faster in the dryer. Guarantee that it will not cause premature baldness in goldfish, cannot cause dental decay, and, if liberally applied, protects the skin from harmful ultra-violet rays. Provided that all these claims are true you will find specialists in each of these areas who will, for a consideration, endorse your claims whole-heartedly.

But if every unit is so incredibly expensive, how, I hear you ask, are you going to sell enough to pay for all this development and promotion. The secret lies in stage two; the production breakthrough. Before the hope and euphoria which greet your announce-ment have reached their peak, follow up with the revelation that, aware of the high cost, your scientists have managed to isolate an inexpensive synthetic substitute which slashes the cost of production. Your main problem will soon be keeping up with demand until the first batch of disappointed complaints filter through. If you then announce to the world that a brand new miracle cure for teenage acne has just been discovered by your researchers working in the Brazilian swamps, the letters will swiftly turn into anxious enquiries as to when it will be commercially available. Repeat the process.

Provided that you move quickly enough from one revolutionary dis-covery to another you will be able to apply for a Nobel Prize. The advant-age if you win is that you will receive a considerable sum of money; the dis-advantage is that it will then be difficult for you to continue in the miracle drug business. Should you win the Prize, however, all is not lost. Use your ex-tensive publicity facilities to announce that you are donating your prize to some worthy cause, then bounce the cheque and vanish from sight. How many Nobel Prize winners have *you* heard of since their award?

19 So you want to have a private army

You will need

A set of uniforms
A parade ground
A shooting range
Shoe polish
Medals

Before You Start

Do bear in mind that soldiers are often rather rough people and use a lot of bad language. Before starting a project of this kind record an hour or so of particularly offensive phrases and sayings on a cassette recorder. Play a few minutes of it each day, gradually extending your listening time until you can hear the whole tape at full volume without flinching, crying or being sick.

Sounding the Charge

Few boys and girls have not dreamed of riding at the head of their very own army, and even fewer have thought of making their dreams come true, but in fact realizing this particular dream is no more than a matter of following a simple sequence of instructions. The first step is organizing the finance, for private armies are expensive to raise, though profitable once they are operational.

The quickest method is to become a king, as you will then be able to raise almost unlimited credit. Do not, however, make the announcement to the world at large. Most people are sceptical about kings who go around pressing the point. If, on the other hand, you take great pains to conceal the fact, bank managers and bookies will fall over themselves to be both generous and discrete. So will restaurant owners. The latter are particularly useful, as once you have recruited your men, the restaurant owners will be able to help you give them meals — and do not forget that an army marches on its stomach. It will help enormously if you are African, but if you are not, learn a few basic Spanish or Portuguese phrases instead.

Once you have acquired some funds it will be fairly easy to recruit the basis of an army. In the initial stages you can minimize your overheads by allowing the soldiers to sleep at home until ordered to report for duties and training. Those living some distance away can be billeted in your own house until you can afford some barracks. At all stages, discipline is absolutely essential; there is little point in taking on a war if none of the soldiers will follow you. You will only make yourself upset and an upset commander loses battles!

Severe breaches of discipline can be punished by having the miscreants shot, but unless you are

Raising your own private army is surprisingly easy once you have spent some time considering details. There are places all over the world where potential soldiers are looking for jobs yet need very little in return except for a square meal once or twice a day. Recruitment out of the way, you can do as much marching about and saluting as you like.

Here is a suggested uniform incorporating all sorts of useful accessories. Of particular interest are the high explosive boots for clearing land-mines.

fortunate enough to be based on an uninhabited island, take care to shoot quietly as it is frowned upon in many places.

Equipment is the next objective and it is advisable to read up on the subject before ordering anything. There are plenty of adequate books in any good bookshop and study could help you avoid a costly error. Make sure that the small arms are powerful enough to be effective. Pellet guns, though good value, do not have the necessary punch for normal combat.

Resist the temptation to buy up private collections, for it is often impossible to obtain the correct ammunition and there are cheaper ways of equipping your army with clubs. A handy guide for checking that ammunition ordered is correct for your weapons is to measure the diameter of the bullet at its widest point, then compare with the diameter of the barrel. If they match, the ammunition is probably correct. (Do not measure the bullet across the base of the cartridge case. This often has a little lip to stop the bullet sliding down the barrel before firing.) The same principle can be applied to artillery shells and mortar bombs. Landmines, though useful, are best avoided. They are almost invisible when correctly placed and it is only too easy to forget where your men have put them.

When purchasing tanks and other military vehicles, make certain that they have been properly serviced and

It is essential, when ordering ammunition, to make sure that it will fit your weapons. Included here is a handy, make-it-yourself bullet measurer. Place the head of the bullet in each hole in turn until you find the one which fits best. Read off the corresponding measurement when you are placing your order.

Key to bullet guide

A .303 Martini Henry 1902 Hand-Tooled Replica
B Sawn-off Shotgun
C .22 Hi-power Potato Gun
D .28ish Homemade
E 18″ Howitzer (ladies model)
F 55″ Oerlikon Unisex Repeater
G 300mm Krupps Wunderbar Slogger
H 20ft Self-Seeking Naval Torpedo (requires submarine attachment)
I 4″ pocket crossbow (collapsible model)
J Size 4 knitting needle (see chapter 5)

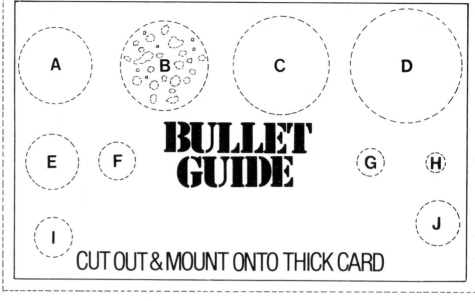

BULLET GUIDE

CUT OUT & MOUNT ONTO THICK CARD

have no shot holes in them or they will leak when fording deep streams or puddles. Listen to the engines for any tell-tale rattles or rumblings and have a look at the oil dipstick. If the oil has a streaky or emulsified appearance there is a good chance that the head gasket is going and repairs could be expensive. Finally, test the suspension by bouncing each corner, looking for the excessive travel that indicates advanced wear. Any clanking coming from the moving tracks may be irritating on long journeys, but is quite usual.

Your troops should be regularly drilled, and most armies carry out drills by numbers. If each man shouts out a number for each part of a sequence it serves to fix the drill in his mind and encourages that sought-after crispness of performance. You can abandon this technique once the men are off duty so that they can talk and get to know each other. It is also advisable to dispense with it when they are in combat, particularly if they are operating behind the lines. Get them used to working as a team by making

There are lots of boot styles to choose from and it is primarily a matter of personal taste. The shamrock sole design shown on the right is great fun and will give your men confidence.

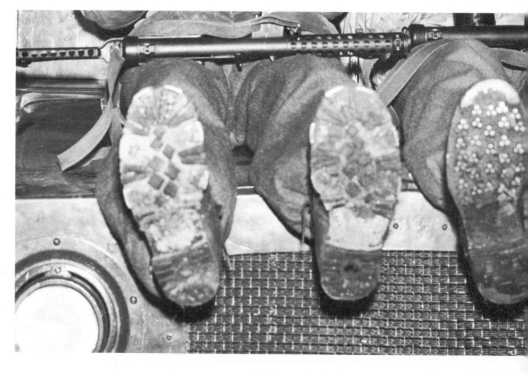

112

them march together in the same direction. The same principle should be encouraged on the firing range.

Your own appearance and bearing should be the standard to which your men should aspire so always make sure that you are neatly turned out yourself. Sleep with your legs under the mattress so that their creases help keep those in your trousers razor-sharp, and have your boots chromium-plated. They will then only require a quick buff-up to set a gleaming example to the ranks. Do not, under any circumstances, wear fish-net stockings except in the officers' mess unless they are a standard part of the uniform.

Once your army is trained and equipped you can begin looking for work. Read the newspapers every day to keep abreast of world affairs and to look out for any emerging ethnic or political groups that could use some extra firepower. Learn a little about politics as this will stand you in good stead when considering an enquiry. There is little advantage in allying yourself with a losing side unless you can take advantage of a rout to pick up some extra equipment.

A useful tip if forced to join a precipitous retreat is to run slightly slower than the soldiers of the army to which you are attached until you

To reduce costs it is quite possible to adapt one of your civilian lounge suits as a parade uniform and any competent tailor will be able to knock up something pretty spectacular in an hour or two.

113

are a decent enough distance behind them to start shooting at them. At the same time send radio messages to the advancing enemy to hurry up and relieve you as you're getting low on ammunition. This tactical principle underlines the importance of knowing your enemy, particularly the names of the senior officers and their wives. Most commanders and their senior staff are very tired after a major engagement and would feel well disposed towards you if you were able to issue invitations to a quietly relaxing victory ball where they could unwind.

If you have done your homework well you should find yourself on the winning side, which not only means that you should be able to get your bill settled, but also offers the possibility of other rewards. If it is a fairly small war in a small country, you may even be given control of the army in gratitude for your vital assistance. In such instances it is usually possible to use the army for a little freelancing to supplement your commander's salary.

If you make sure that the borrowed soldiers are amply rewarded out of the spoils of your enterprises they truly will appreciate you. This is no bad thing as it opens up the possibility of organizing your own Coup d'Etat and ousting the regime in order to take control of the country and its resources. It is then entirely possible to declare yourself king and start the whole process again on a

Choosing a uniform is not as simple as you may think as it has to be suitable for all sorts of circumstances. The uniform shown here is quite adaptable and efficient but can be a handicap when running through spiky undergrowth or jumping out of trees.

much grander scale. You will find finance even easier to raise and can begin playing the world's major political blocs off against each other until you have enough arms and equipment to begin taking over some of the nearby states.

Once you have a few of these conquests under your belt, you can declare yourself an emperor. Emperors can raise even greater assistance than kings and you will soon be able to set up your own arms manufacturing facilities, which will strengthen your position considerably. Provided that you retain close control over your expanding forces, and are careful not to oppress those you conquer too severely, you will be well on your way to world domination. You will then have sufficient resources to consider attacking other planets and writing your memoirs.

The four Glorious Last Moments devised by Wing Surgeon Adolf 'Geronimo' Markowitz (centre). Anticlockwise from bottom right: the 'David Niven' parachute drop into enemy fortress; the Custer, an evergreen favourite; the Light Brigade Special, for the grand occasion; and the 'John Wayne' Wetleg Sprint — last man on the beach is a sissy.

COMPLETE KAMIKAZE COURSE

You will need
_____
A white silk scarf
Goggles
A bicycle
A sense of Destiny

A professional kamikaze in action. Note the effective use of smoke and flames.

Before You Start

Make sure that you are in reasonable physical condition as kamikaze work is quite exacting. Devote a few minutes each day to callisthenics and spiritual contemplation. Both regimens can be performed simultaneously if you are pressed for time.

The air of quiet determination, the noble posture and the spark of selfless courage in the eyes single him out from the crowd. There is a firm resolution in his stride, and one senses that he sees horizons beyond the view of ordinary folk. Women swoon at his passing, and strong men make way for him. Perhaps it is something in the set of his jaw, the hint of steel behind the gentle calm, that marks him out as a kamikaze pilot.

One of the most important aspects of the basic training schedule is learning to overcome the hesitation factor that most people experience when setting out to terminate their own lives, and unless you can override this reflex there is little point in pursuing this career. You do, in fact, have to re-condition yourself, and it is best to tackle this problem in easy stages. Start by assuming the 'at attention' position, hands gripping the seams of your trousers, chin up and chest pushed out. Count to three, then let yourself fall forwards without changing your position at all. Once you have mastered this, try it from a table-top or the back of a chair until you can execute the manoeuvre without hesitation. Having thus assured yourself that you are able to overcome this basic inhibition, you can begin the second stage of training.

You will need to enrol in your local flying club for one or two lessons. This will be your only major investment but it can be kept to a minimum by reading all you can about the basic techniques of flying before you go for your first lesson. As soon as you have grasped the essential techniques of starting up an aircraft, taxiing, taking off and steering, you can withdraw from the course to concentrate on the other aspects of your training. Learning to land an aircraft is of course unnecessary.

Lifts offer plenty of opportunity for training exercises. (a) While the lift is in motion, position yourself directly in front of the door edges. (b) At the precise moment just before the lift stops and the doors open, begin falling forward. (c) Split-second timing is essential for kamikaze operations. If your timing is right you should hit the floor before the doors are even fully open. (d) Once on the floor, do not delay too long before getting up again. Getting trapped when the doors close again indicates that you are not up to a sufficiently high standard.

First stage in training to be a kamikaze anything is learning emotional discipline and a fixed, dedicated gaze. Movements should all be jerky and neck movements kept to a minimum. Flared nostrils are a useful addition. Beginners may find it easier to cover the whole face in a thin layer of acrylic resin.

Practise bowing repeatedly from the waist by assuming the 'at attention' position once again. This time, instead of crashing to the floor, bend forward until the upper part of your body is parallel to the ground, pause, then resume the starting position. Repeat the process several times in rapid succession. The next thing is to cultivate a taste for saki. Start by filling an empty saki flask with water and practice pouring small nips into a little bowl and drinking it in a single fluid movement without any alteration of facial expression. The function of this exercise is two-fold. In addition to teaching you to drink in a noble fashion, it is one of the first exercises in inscrutability.

A complete lack of expression is extremely hard to achieve, but do not despair if you cannot manage it satisfactorily, for there are ways round the problem. A useful tip is to coat your face in a mixture of starch and transparent latex to limit the amount of muscle movement. If this is still insufficient, a foolproof alternative is to prepare some acrylic resin, which is not only completely transparent but is also extremely hard and durable. Leave holes for the mouth, nose and eyes, spreading the mixture evenly over the rest of the face. Allow half-an-hour and your facial musculature will be entirely and effectively immobilized. You will need only to polish your face every week or so to prevent a build up of dust, but do not overdo it as the result will be a rather disconcerting high-gloss finish.

You are now ready to begin the final stage of training, for which an inexpensive bicycle will be required. Roller skates can be used in emergencies but are not quite as desirable as they lack the desired weight and size. After familiarizing yourself with the local topography, select a suitable starting point for your dummy mission and wait there on the bike for the arrival of your target; a public bus is ideal. While waiting you can practise the traditional high-pitched Banzai! screams used as a battlecry, but do this under your breath to avoid attracting premature attention.

Once the target bus is in sight, place your foot on the pedal, grip the handlebars firmly, and unless you are employing the resin technique, adopt your most inscrutable expression. Immediately prior to take off, adopt the bowing position with your head projecting well in front of the handlebars and pedal furiously at the side of the approaching bus to attain maximum speed before impact. Do make absolutely sure that you have allowed for the forward motion of the bus when determining your time of launch. There can be no greater blow to your pride than hurtling at breakneck speed past the rear of the target, and in addition you risk being seriously injured by any traffic going in the opposite direction.

Once this exercise has been faultlessly executed, your training is complete and you are ready to take on your first and, if correctly performed, last assignment. It is now simply a

Girls either swoon or go slightly fuzzy round the edges in the presence of kamikaze men. Here we see one in the process of doing both.

Watching *Away All Boats* with Jeff Chandler several times will give you lots of useful tips, and probably a severe headache. It is often suggested that Jeff Chandler himself was an experienced kamikaze and was bitterly disappointed at having to play the captain. This view is supported by this still from the film.

Once you have mastered the basic techniques you can begin field exercises. Bus ramming with a bicycle is a good test of skill. Pick a good launch point and watch for a moving bus in the nearside lane. As soon as it has reached point A in the accompanying diagram, lower your head until your nose touches the handlebars and the top of your head extends level with the front wheel. Pedal as fast as you can in order to make maximum contact with the side of the vehicle at point B.

matter of awaiting a suitable pretext. As this may occur at any time, it is best to be fully equipped and kitted up at all times. The actual pretext itself can be quite small provided that it can be construed as a matter of personal honour. Being short-changed at the local store, having credit refused, being pestered by the dog next door — all are perfectly adequate.

Having performed the preliminary rituals, cycle to the nearest aerodrome, enter the first aircraft that is fuelled, go through the starting procedure and taxi to the take-off point. Whilst preparing to take off, you can practise one or two Banzais! before getting airborne. Once you are up, complete silence should be maintained until the final stage of the mission. When you are in sight of your target, take a deep breath and issue your very best Banzai! as you push the stick forward and open the throttle.

At this point it is worth noting some of the special effects that will add an extra touch of style. Plunging to your final meeting with fate in a fiercely burning aircraft is one of the classic techniques, but it requires a little advance preparation. If you cannot arrange for the required amount of spare fuel with which to douse the plane prior to take-off, a cheap and easy alternative is to take a strip of

bright red cloth approximately twenty-five feet long and three to four feet wide. Using a pair of good-quality dressmaking scissors cut several long, slender V-shapes from one end to about half-way along. This can then be neatly rolled up and carried to the aircraft. Shortly before the final impact, unroll the cloth and allow it to hang out of the cockpit and trail behind, where it will flutter wildly to provide a reasonable alternative to actual flames. For visual reference you can do no better that to watch *Away All Boats,* starring Jeff Chandler, several times, taking notes.

Even if you find it a real problem to obtain an aircraft on the day, do not give up the idea too soon. Modern hang-gliders are relatively inexpensive and provide an easily obtainable and fairly effective substitute. Plunging in flames is, however, slightly less desirable when using these craft, as you run the risk of using up your craft before you have completed your final approach, with regrettable and disappointing results.

One final word: resist the temptation to proclaim memorable last words as you plummet downwards. Such utterings as 'Mother!' or 'Take this, you abomination!' do little to uphold the noble traditions of the Warriors of the Divine Wind.

X MIRROR, Friday, August 16, 1940.

Daily Mirror

ONE PENNY

No. 11,441
Registered at the G.P.O. as a Newspaper.

KAMIKAZE ASSAULT
144
cycle-borne raiders blasted in street battles

A HUNDRED AND FORTY - FOUR ENEMY RAIDERS WERE BROUGHT DOWN UP TO MIDNIGHT YESTERDAY.

That was Britain's answer at the end of the day of the greatest air attacks of the war, in which the German "blitz" swept the length of Britain.

Twenty-seven R.A.F. fighters were lost in the mighty defence battles, but eight of the pilots are safe.

For hour after hour through the day, and then into the night, our fighters swept against the huge raiding squadrons.

The German Air Force used more than a thousand bombers and fighters in the attacks.

Croydon Aerodrome, London's airport before the war, was raided last night. "Bombs were dropped on and around the aerodrome," said the Air Ministry later. "Some damage was done, but details are not yet available."

Sirens were sounded in a wide area of Greater London.

Many towns were attacked during the day, and a number of people killed. German aerodromes in the south-east and in the north-east were bombed.

Heavy attacks on south-east areas went on into the evening hours. All the time German machines were being shot out of the sky.

Over one coast district R.A.F. fighters and the guns smashed up a three-hour attack by 250 raiders.

Once again there was a spell in which German planes were dropping out of the sky at the rate of one a minute.

14 Dive-Bombers

At another point the destruction of several barrage balloons cost nine raiders. People in yet another district saw eight of a big attacking squadron destroyed.

It was the most gruelling day for the R.A.F. fighters. And their greatest.

Fourteen dive-bombers, protected by fighters, attacked Croydon Aerodrome. High explosive "screamers" and incendiary bombs were dropped. Some people were killed and a number injured.

The raiders were first seen when they started to dive about three miles from the aerodrome. People in the streets saw them come to a few hundred feet before the bombs were released.

Within a few seconds anti-aircraft guns put up a fierce barrage. Three of the raiders are believed to have been smashed.

One bomb narrowly missed a gas-works, but houses in an adjoining road were hit.

Main casualties of the raid were caused by a bomb which wrecked a building where men were working.

Hours afterwards rescue workers were still digging in the debris for bodies of the victims.

Not far away a bomb dropped only a few yards from a bus and blew out a loft, wide crater. Passengers were injured by flying glass as all the bus windows were blown out. Part of the engine was

Contd. on Back Page, Col. 2

SUPPLY MUDDLE: OFFICIAL

WAR production is frequently left to face not merely competition between the Ministries, but even between different departments of the same Ministry—all pressing for orders to be completed.

This criticism of the lack of co-ordination in the present system of priority of supplies is made by the Select Committee on National Expenditure in a report issued last night.

A contractor told the committee that—if he followed every order he received about the urgency of various articles—he would have his shops full of half-finished stuff, owing to continued switching from one job to another.

The committee recommend that the priority organisation, the Raw Materials Department and the Salvage Organisation should be separated from the Ministry of Supply and placed under a separate Minister or a Parliamentary Secretary to the Minister of Defence.

This new and compact department would not be a user of any of the materials handled and would be able to allocate them to the best possible use.

Increased Costs

Unless rapid decisions are taken, the committee say, delays in production and increased costs are inevitable.

Whatever new organisation is adopted, it must command the respect of all departments and have overriding powers.

If factories are to be kept at greatest production with least cost it is suggested both planning and priority periods should as far as possible be for not less than three months.

The committee heard evidence from Mr. Arthur Greenwood, Minister without Portfolio, who presides over the Production Committee of the Cabinet, and Colonel J. J. Llewellin, in charge of the Central Priority Department of the Ministry of Supply.

PARACHUTES A VAIN NAZI RUSE

THE dropping of parachutes by enemy aircraft during the night of August 13 was no more than a clumsy effort, on the part of the enemy to undermine the British moral, the Ministry of Information said last night.

A large number of parachutes were dropped in widely-separated areas.

In many instances the harness had not been undone and in some places empty parachutes were seen falling.

In addition, bags containing instructions purporting to be operation orders were found. At least one bag was dropped in a place and under circumstances which make it obvious that the Germans intended the bag to fall into the hands of the military authorities.

Contd. on Back Page, Col. 4

This bus was damaged in the Croydon raid.

Plane Trap Is Secret

A PLANE trap erected by the Ministry of Transport caught a German bomber yesterday and wrecked it.

All the crew were killed.

British military authorities have no intention of giving away to the enemy details of the plane trap.

The trap is the latest British "hush-hush" defence weapon, as the Nazis have already learned to their cost.

More news of its formidable and effective nature can be expected soon.

Threw Bomb Overboard

When a German raider dropped a bomb down the funnel of a trawler in the Channel, the skipper ran from the bridge, carried the bomb from the engine-room to the deck, and threw it overboard.

It exploded a second before it hit the water, and the ship was undamaged.

The skipper's courage saved the ship and the lives of all but one of his crew.

He picked the bomb from the bilge, and staggered with it up the companion-way.

TRAIN BOMBED: SEVERAL KILLED

SEVERAL passengers were killed by bomb splinters when a train was stopped during a raid over north-east England yesterday.

In the same area an express train was machine-gunned by a German plane.

A passenger, David Stafford, was injured in the leg. Carriage windows were broken.

GLOSSARY

Multiply Your Friends with Home Cloning

Aardvark An improbable creature whose prey is particularly easy to clone. The uncommonly close resemblance of one ant to another suggests that they are already clones. This is supported by the fact that they behave in an identical fashion *viz.* at picnics.

Fruit Fly An insect whose rapid reproductive rate is used to illustrate genetic principles, evident from the fact that some have brown eyes, some blue and some one of each.

Pipette A small pipe used by French smokers.

An Ocean Going Liner of Your Own

Binnacle Not to be confused with pinnace (q.v.) or pinnacle, it is often made of brass.

Pinnace Not to be confused with Pinafore (q.v.) or pennant, it is a smaller vessel than a liner.

Pinafore (HMS) A ship for transporting singers.

Taxidermy — Stuffing Is Fun

Aardvark A badly stuffed dog with a sticky tongue.

Formaldehyde A close associate of Dr Jekyll.

Horsehair The traditional packing material for stuffing and mounting sofas.

Indoor Ballooning to Competition Standards

Guylines Queues of young men hoping for a ride. They can be used to defray your operating costs.

Hot Air The product of bringing four or more balloonists together in close proximity to a launch site. It is produced in an inverse ratio to the amount of ballooning they have done.

Championship Needlework

Stress Factor The means of calculating structural efficiency. It is also a measurement arising out of regret for starting a large-scale project.

Thimble An emblem or logotype for a society for those with speech impediments.

Wool The outer casing of a sheep.

Sink Like a Stone in Your Own Bathysphere

Fathom To understand something in terms of a man's average height, e.g. 'I understand that I have gone down three feet, I fathom that I have gone down six feet.'

Reef A type of knot used by sailors, not to be confused with the *relief* of coming up alive.

Submarine Trench A type of overcoat worn at considerable depths in the ocean.

Don't Be Ordinary — You Too Can Break Records

Aardvark A creature holding the record for absurdity of appearance.

Sweetest Thing A record not worth competing for unless you are tiny, fluffy and pink with large blue eyes.

Xylophone An instrument occasionally used on records which soon get broken.

Brain Surgery for Pleasure and Profit

Head The part of the body where the brain is located. Not to be confused with the naval term for lavatory although in some people they are equally applicable.

Needle To make the patient angry. A useful technique as the throbbing veins of apoplexy are easy to locate.

Sympathetic Nerve A similar technique to the above involving genial audacity, as in 'Oh poor you, I can't seem to get the top of your skull on properly.'

Tympani A copper instrument covered in a taut membrane and emitting a resonant throbbing akin to post-operative side-effects.

Create Plunging Vistas with Open-Cast Mining

Boring The sensation experienced during large-scale excavation.

Deposit Small heaps of processed matter left by startled birds and other creatures disturbed during blasting.

Vein A continuous, linear concentration of valuable substances.

Breeding Combat Hamsters

Aardvark One of the many mammals that will pose no real threat to your breeding stock, unless your hamsters are covered in ants and may, as a result, be lashed to death inadvertently.

Cross-breeding A form of controlled mating designed to make your combat animals fighting made. Making loud, unexpected noises at the crucial moment is usually sufficient.

Freeze Your Way to a Fortune with Cryogenics

Absolute Zero Very, very cold as in 'It's absolutely freezing in there.' The point at which it becomes important not to drop or strike your patients to avoid shattering them.

Centigrade An articulated animal popularly supposed to be capable of being sorted into different sizes a hundred ways.

Calvin Scale The small flakes of skin shed by members of a religious sect.

How to Contact the Spirit World

Ectoplasm A sudden and substantial emission of uncertain material from the mouth. This phenomenon is often exhibited during wild drinking bouts.

Medium Mid-way between two extremes. In this context refers to practitioners with half-baked ideas about the afterlife.

Spirit Guide A mystical entity associated with the post-death world which acts as a guide to the medium. The degree of contact is termed the *spirit level.*

Orbital Hardware from the Home Workshop

Countdown The measuring of elapsed time prior to launch. Not to be confused with discount, which you can offer your customers.

Reactor One who reacts one who acts again if they got it wrong the first time.

Nuclear Pertaining to the use of atomic physics to initiate an immensely powerful controlled explosion, as in nuclear family, when the male parent comes home drunk after spending all the housekeeping yet again.

Terminal Speed The speed at which you're almost certain to kill yourself.

Save Cash with Hydro-Electrics

Ammeter One who devours ham with his mouth full.

High Tension The experience undergone by those suffering from acrophobia.

Commutator A word similar to computer, meaning one who travels to work by public transportation.

Direct Current Certain types of berry that do not mince words. Matters appertaining to current, or a close relationship with same are described as current affairs.

Convert Your Home to a Romantic Ruin

Aardvark A predator to be discouraged if you intend to introduce a termite colony to weaken structural timbers.

Guttering Exhibiting fluttering movements as in a candle. This should be encouraged in houses intended to become ruins as it weakens the fabric of the structure, and precipitates a romantic film of plaster dust.

Tenon Saw A joiner's jointing saw not to be confused with the surgeon's instrument for sawing joints, the tendon saw.

Nouvelle Cuisine Terminale

Artichoke A spiny, multi-petalled vegetable for sucking butter from.

Crescendo The expression of creative temperament, often accompanied by hurling of pans and dishes.

Sauce An impertinent relish often associated with saucisson, itself an important part of Cuisine Terminale as, literally translated, it means a long tube of gunpowder for firing a charge.

Sauté The past participle of the French verb *sauter,* to leap. The recipe for springing potatoes seems to have been lost.

Like Big Cars and Trench Coats? Be a Racketeer

Gat Slang for a handgun. Sometimes known as a rod when shooting fish.

Liquor Usually made at night (moonshine) and so awful that the government made it illegal. Puts hair on the chest, hence many racketeers were called gorillas.

Speakeasy One who does not talk out of the corner of the mouth, i.e. an outsider.

Nobel Prize Here I Come!

Centrifuge A place where 100 people hide.

Retort A snappy answer. Useful to have if official tests are unfavourable.

Saline Deposit Proceeds salted away in a Swiss account.

Saline Drip Crocodile tears when facing an official enquiry.

So You Want to Have a Private Army?

Corporal Punishment Smacking badly behaved NCOs.

Ground Attack The assaulting of certain strategic or tactical objectives; hills, woods, rivers etc. Sometimes done despite the presence of enemy troops.

Shell A large calibre projectile in which you can hear the sea. They are usually inscribed with people's names. Sometimes dropped on unsuspecting troops by airship; hence barrage balloon.

Trench Foot A linear measure by which the extent of defence works are assessed.

Complete Kamikaze Course

Aardvark A legendary battlecry never knowingly used by the select Divine Wind pilots.

Divine Wind A not unpleasant form of flatulence sometimes used for finding hidden water sources.

Jeff Chandler A man who shouts at Kamikaze pilots.

The scream of engines in their final dive to glory. The scream of engines in their final dive to glory.

ADVANCED PROJECTS

For those who hanker after something a little more challenging a list of advanced projects is set out below. Do not attempt any of these unless you have already gained some experience in the projects already described herein. Experience and the ability to improvise are essential to the success of most of the following schemes.

Causing a Recession

Adversely affecting national economies involves a great deal of hard work and the help of Trade Union leaders and Captains of Industry will, with their considerable experience, be most useful in speeding up the process. Learn how to accelerate inflation, over-value currencies, curtail investment and see the numbers of jobless rise dramatically.

Open Your Own Swiss Bank

You too can be a gnome, hi-hoing down to your overflowing vaults. All you need is a few photographs of the Swiss Alps and a terrible memory for names to get the punters rolling in. They pay *you* interest for the privilege of letting you keep the money that they don't dare to withdraw and spend.

Discover the Secret of Perpetual Motion

Resolve the energy problem and get rich as well as enormously famous. All you need to do is to find a way of initiating motion which, when underway, will sustain its own motion.

Build Your Own Electron Microscope

The technology already exists, and with determination, a soldering iron and an electron microscope kit, you too can see tiny things.

Re-covering Bald Pets with Bumble Bee Hides

This revolutionary idea is quite revolutionary, and can revolutionize the lives of thousands of bald pets. All you need is a scalpel, a pair of

tweezers and 100,000,000,000,000 bees. It will also revolutionize the lives of the bees.

A Bridge from London to New York Built Out of Used Matches?

'Impossible,' you may cry! 'It cannot be done,' you may declare — and we are inclined to agree.

FURTHER READING

Keep your Brain Warm: Grow your Hair Inwards
A scientifically researched book of practical hints and tips by a panel of woolly thinkers. Illustrated chapters describe and analyse such topics as doing without sunglasses by letting your hair grow over the front of your brain. Not recommended for bald men.

200 Brain-Bursting Ideas by Dr. Roger Megaton
Essential reading for anyone given to inserting explosives in ear, nose or throat.
Each step-by-step project comes with a damp sponge and a small bottle of disinfectant.

SRAEY 02
NAHT SSEL
NI SDRAW—
KCAB DAER
OT NRAEL

200 BRAIN BURSTING IDEAS

Doctor Roger Megaton

Keep Your Brain Warm Grow your hair inwards

PINNACLES OF FUTILITY

Ima.P.Nutt

INDEX